LOVE
YOUR LUNCHES

LOVE YOUR LUNCHES

vibrant & healthy recipes
to brighten up your day

Bec Dickinson

hardie grant books

CONTENTS

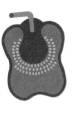

1

INTRODUCTION

LUNCH IS AT THE HEART of our days. The mid-work sanctuary, where we find a well-justified moment of rest, recuperation, and most importantly, a chance to dig into little boxes of daily fuel.

There's no underestimating the power of a delicious, impending lunch. It works as a propeller to push us through the morning yawn and cups of tea, onto our well-deserved and highly anticipated meal. Long gone are the days of the soggy cheese white-bread sandwiches that donned the squashed imprints of the insides of our bag. Lunch envy has become a true reality, and the pain of being the onlooker (smeller... and scavenger) of another's carefully packed food is enough to send us back to the kitchen and dreaming of a better meal... as we stab the dry salad we bought at the local supermarket.

We are always told not to skip breakfast, but at some point lunch has become a fallback for which we rely on the sandwich shops or the questionable two-minute mac 'n' cheese.

But no longer! It's time to reclaim our lunch break. Let's provide ourselves with something to look forward to, and brighten our days right when we need it most, with meals that are fresh and sustaining and will nourish you from the inside out.

This book has got something to suit a varying range of time contraints, budgets and tastes. It's all about bringing back the packed lunch, but this time, in a more celebrated form. Most recipes can be adapted to suit what's available at hand, and while some methods do require a little bit more time than a ready-made salad or soup from your local deli, your energy levels, tastebuds, and hungry work colleagues will thank you for it.

PLANNING AHEAD

ONE OF THE KEY COMPONENTS TO LOCK IN A SUCCESSFUL WEEK OF PACKED LUNCHES IS PREPARING AHEAD. WHILST THIS MAY SOUND LIKE A TEDIOUS TASK THAT ONLY THE HEAVILY ORGANISED PARTAKE IN, ONCE YOU GET INTO A ROUTINE, IT'S EASY!

WEEKLY MENU

To save a night-before rush, use the therapeutic minutes of the weekend to flick through these pages and mark anything that jumps out at you. Write a list and note the recipes that make multiple servings so you can roll them over into a few days of lunches. Is there anything you've previously frozen ahead? It's time to utilise all your freezer ammunition, and use up any sad-looking vegetables. Find a recipe to slot them into and hail this chance to get creative with your cooking.

Knowing the weather forecast for the week will not only ensure you have an umbrella at dire times, but also help you anticipate what food you'll be in the mood for, as nothing is quite as disorientating as a hot soup on a sweltering day. Your planning can even take into account the weeks to come with frozen meals. Have some Red Lentil, Squash & Coconut Dhal (page 24) for lunch one day, and freeze ahead for the next month. This planning may even soon become your favourite way to spend your Sunday afternoons... you've been warned.

SHOPPING LISTS

Once you've written out the lunch meals for the week, to save on money and waste, consult the fridge and pantry first. The majority of grains in the book can be substituted for whatever alternative you have available, and starchy vegetables and leafy greens are usually interchangeable. A list will help you stay on track in the supermarket, and avoid any impulse buys. As a bonus, you'll also save on multiple trips to the shops, meaning more time in the kitchen! Add any 'must-purchase' staples that have been used up to your list, so you're already one step closer to preparing your next meal with ease.

MAKING EXTRA

Being ahead of the lunch bandwagon can be as simple as making a little extra at mealtimes to ensure ease when putting your lunch together. This can be cooking extra vegetables for your Sunday roast (perfect for the Homemade Bento Box on page 68) or quickly simmering some grains on the hob, which freeze perfectly and are ready to go after defrosting in the microwave or in the fridge overnight.

Never underestimate these small advancements; your Monday self will thank you for it when lunch is effortlessly placed into a container, ready to go. During the preparation for the week ahead, make sure you allow a little time to make your afternoon snacks. The Matcha, Almond & Raspberry Bliss Balls (page 84), are simply blitzed and can sit in the fridge awaiting a trip to work – unless you eat them all beforehand (no judgment).

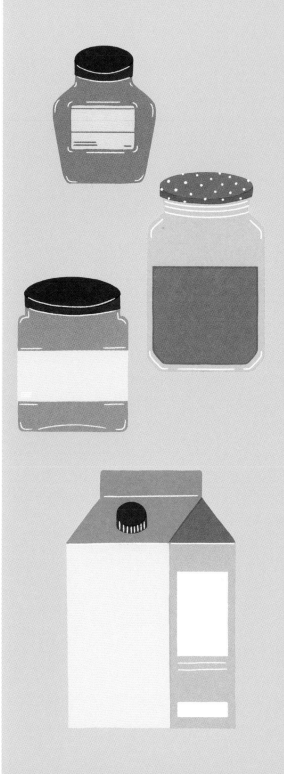

THE STAPLES

Having a key set of ingredients ready to go in your kitchen and your desk drawer is the full set of ammo you will need to make you the master of successful lunches. In this book, there is a chapter dedicated to maintaining staples and using those cupboard odds and ends (page 92). While it may seem a bit of a drag to purchase something you won't use immediately, it is the essence of investment cooking, and looking out for your future hungry self. Keep an eye on when to refill your ingredient stock and always double-check before shopping (being caught without lemons is a scary reality). Once you're in the 'staples sync', you'll build up a prized range of ingredients at your disposal.

While we all have a slightly different array of must-have ingredients in our own kitchens, here's a helpful list to inspire a range of staples to suit a variety of lunches. Once stored in your kitchen, you won't know how you cooked without them.

CUPBOARD
bread (pita, rye, soda, wholewheat)
dark chocolate (70% cocoa solids)
dried fruit (apricots, dates, sultanas)
flour (buckwheat, plain, wholewheat)
nut selection (almonds, hazelnuts, peanuts)
rolled oats
seeds (pumpkin, sesame, sunflower, pine nuts)

TINNED
black beans
cannellini beans
chickpeas (garbanzo beans)
sardines
sweetcorn
tomatoes
tuna

JARRED
clear honey
miso paste
mustard
nut butter
olives
passata
peppers
pesto
sun-dried tomatoes (in oil)
tahini
tomato purée (paste)

GRAINS & PASTA
barley
buckwheat
bulgur wheat
couscous
fresh and dried lentils (green, red)
pasta (regular, spelt, wholewheat)
quinoa
rice (basmati, brown, wild)

DRIED HERBS & SPICES

bay leaves
black peppercorns
cayenne pepper
chilli flakes
cumin seeds
dukkah
garam masala
ground cinnamon
ground nutmeg
ground turmeric
harrissa paste
medium curry powder
oregano
paprika (smoked, sweet)
rosemary
sea salt
sumac
thyme
za'tar

FRUIT, VEGETABLES & GREENS

apples
avocados
bananas
carrots
cauliflower
chillies
garlic
ginger
leafy greens (kale, rocket, spinach)
lemons
limes
mushrooms
onions (brown, red)
pears
peppers (bell peppers)
potatoes (normal, sweet)
tomatoes

FREEZER

bacon or pancetta
mixed berries
overripe bananas (peeled and chopped)
pastry (filo, puff, shortcrust)
pre-made soups
sliced bread
stock (chicken, meat, vegetable)

FRIDGE

butter (salted, unsalted)
cheese (Cheddar, cottage cheese, feta,
Parmesan)
eggs
fresh herbs (basil, coriander/cilantro,
parsley, mint)
Greek or natural yoghurt
milk

OILS, VINEGAR & SAUCES

apple cider vinegar
balsamic vinegar
olive oil
rice vinegar
sesame oil
sherry vinegar
soy sauce
Tabasco sauce
wine vinegar (red, white)
Worcestershire sauce

DESK DRAWER ESSENTIALS

*YOUR SECRET WEAPON TO ACHIEVING
ULTIMATE LUNCH ENVY FROM YOUR
COLLEAGUES, IS TO HAVE A DESK
DRAWER 'PANTRY' FILLED WITH A
FEW SPECIAL INGREDIENTS TO
SPRUCE UP YOUR LUNCHES AND
TRANSFORM ANY OLD MEAL INTO
SOMETHING THAT TICKLES ALL
YOUR TASTEBUDS.*

Fill a small jar with simple and
versatile dressings and olive oil – to
save on a potential daily spill on the
way to work – perfect to top your salads,
bento boxes or to pour over your pasta.

Dried herbs are instant flavour
boosters. Toss oregano, dukkah, chilli
flakes and thyme into your lunch, or
add them to your dressings to
customise them to suit your meal.

Nuts and nut butter are ideal to
sprinkle over your meal, or to simply
snack on when milky tea won't do the
trick. Salted peanuts, almonds, pine
nuts and cashews are perfectly
versatile. Smear almond or peanut
butter on a banana (topped with your
carefully stored mixed seeds) to make
a perfect mid-morning snack.

Use plates and bowls to add to the
lunch experience, instead of hunching
over a small lunch box or tupperware.
This will add a little class to your
restful midday break.

Salt and freshly ground black pepper –
never underestimate the power of
seasoning.

A seed mix of lightly toasted pumpkin,
sunflower and sesame seeds will add
the perfect crunch to any salad.

ESSENTIAL EQUIPMENT

YOU WON'T NEED ANY SPECIALIST EQUIPMENT TO MAKE LOTS OF LOVELY LUNCHES; A FEW BASICS WILL HAVE YOU ON YOUR WAY.

Here are the tools that I use the most to help save time and prepare a wide range of dishes. Lunchtime preparation will never be dull again.

FOOD PROCESSOR
The quickest shortcut to grating and blitzing with speed. Pesto, hummus, cauliflower rice, grated carrot, all done in seconds. This appliance will never get dusty.

HAND-HELD ELECTRIC BLENDER
Save on washing-up and blend soup straight in the pan. Also great for whizzing up smoothies and beating eggs. Not to mention, quite fun to use.

NON-STICK FRYING PAN (SKILLET)
With a large surface area, it's perfect for sautéeing vegetables such as mushrooms, cooking sauces, crisping up fritters (page 112) and lots more. A good-quality non-stick frying pan will last for ages and give healthier results (less oil required) – making it well worth the investment.

MICROPLANE GRATER

You'll wonder how you ever got by without this. Perfect to grate garlic, so it's minced in seconds, quickly create fine citrus zest, and help you achieve the fluffiest grated Parmesan ever.

VEGETABLE PEELER

Not just for potatoes. I use mine mostly for ribboning courgettes (zucchinis) and carrots, to get a fine, delicate texture that will also cut down cooking time. Not to mention, such daintily cut vegetables make for a killer finish for your salads.

SEALED GLASS JARS

Glass jars are the perfect storage tool for your fridge and cupboards and to keep garnishes fresh. Use to store homemade pestos, sauces and dressings. For another use, whip them out for your Lunch in a Jar (pages 62–67).

LUNCH CONTAINERS

THE SATISFACTION OF MAKING YOUR LUNCH FROM SCRATCH AT HOME SHOULD NEVER BE TAINTED BY IT GETTING DESTROYED AMONGST THE HUSTLE AND BUSTLE ON THE TREK TO WORK. THE SPECIAL CARGO NEEDS THE RIGHT CONTAINERS AND PACKAGING TO SAFELY TRANSPORT FROM A TO B.

FLAT-LIDDED AIRTIGHT BOXES

Never ruin a carefully crafted meal by lying it on its side. Invest in a good-quality airtight, lidded lunch box (microwave-proof if you are going to reheat your lunch) that can lie flat in the bottom of your bag, so it can sleep tight on the commute. Also keep your eye out for a multi-compartment box, which will prevent the dreaded sogginess, and leave final assembly to the work desk or kitchen.

FOOD FLASK

In the emergency situation of no available microwave, or simply a willingness to drink straight from the container, a food flask will be your best friend. A good-quality flask should keep your food hot for almost a full workday. The key is to preheat it – simply fill with boiling water and leave for 10 minutes, empty it and then add your lunch. Want a hot lunch at 3.30 p.m.? No problem!

STACKED STAINLESS STEEL

For the more stylish luncher, you can compartmentalise all the different components, including your afternoon snack, and garnishes. Stainless steel is also chemical-free and won't affect or retain any of the flavours of the meal. Perfect for al fresco lunches, too.

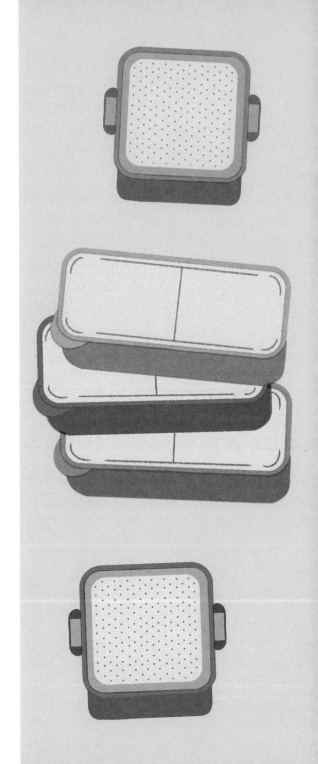

A NOTE ON FREEZING

YOUR LUNCH HAS JUST BEEN LOVINGLY MADE, NOW THE LAST THING YOU WANT TO DO IS RUIN YOUR 'READY-MADE' MEAL EXCITEMENT BY LOSING IT IN THE DEPTHS OF THE FREEZER.

First things first – preparing your lunch for the freezer. This is the simple task of portioning out your meal into sealable containers or cutting your frittata into wedges (rather then coming to the sad realisation that you have to cut it once it is frozen… not easy). If you have a small freezer, swap out containers for bags and lay them flat, so they freeze in perfect portion sizes ready to go.

Next up is labelling. All you need is a permanent marker to quickly jot down the date and what meal it is you've made. There's no time for any surprise frozen tomato sauce when in fact you were expecting the Smoky Paprika Baked Beans (page 102). The date is important for simply eating what has been in the freezer longest and to tell you how old the meal is.

When it comes to defrosting, to make sure your lunch is safe to eat, take your chosen meal out of the freezer and leave in the fridge overnight to defrost. Then when you arrive at lunchtime, reheat it in the microwave for a couple of minutes, stirring halfway, until piping hot. Alternatively, if you have a stove available, it is perfect for reheating certain meals such as soup.

Preparing ahead to get ahead. There is no comfort quite as sweet as the knowledge of a meal already made, waiting in the freezer for you, so you can hit the snooze button just once more. Right before serving, sprinkle with a few fresh garnishes and you're good to go. These recipes are also dinner-perfect, so leftovers can be frozen until needed for lunch – two meals, with half the effort!

FROZEN AHEAD

RED LENTIL, SQUASH & COCONUT DHAL

DHAL IS THE DEFINITION OF COMFORT IN A BOWL. FOR EXTRA TEXTURE AND NOURISHMENT I'VE ADDED KALE AND SERVED IT WITH A SPRINKLING OF PUMPKIN SEEDS.

VEGETARIAN | VEGAN | GLUTEN-FREE | DAIRY-FREE | MAKES 4–6 LUNCH PORTIONS

850 g (1 lb 14 oz/5½ cups) butternut squash, peeled and cut into small cubes (around 2 cm/¾ in)

90 ml (3 fl oz) olive oil

2 brown onions, finely diced

3 garlic cloves, minced

1 tbsp grated fresh ginger

½ tbsp ground cumin

2 tsp ground turmeric

1 tsp garam masala

½ tsp cayenne pepper

2 litres (3½ pints) vegetable stock

400 ml (13 fl oz) coconut milk

400 g (14 oz/1⅔ cups) red lentils, uncooked, rinsed and drained

2 heaped tbsp roughly chopped coriander (cilantro), plus extra to garnish

100 g (3½ oz/2½ cups) kale, roughly chopped

salt and freshly ground black pepper

pumpkin seeds, to garnish

1 Preheat the oven to 200°C (400°F/ Gas 6). Line a baking tray with baking parchment. On the tray toss together the squash and 60 ml (2 fl oz) of the oil, season and roast for 15 minutes, stirring half way through.

2 Meanwhile, heat the remaining oil in a large saucepan over a medium heat, then add the onions and cook for 4 minutes or until softened and translucent. Stir in the garlic, ginger, and all the dried spices, and cook for a further 2 minutes or until the spices are aromatic.

3 Pour in the stock, coconut milk and red lentils. Bring to the boil, then stir in the roasted butternut squash. Reduce to a simmer and leave to bubble away for 30 minutes, (stirring occasionally, scraping the bottom of the pan), or until the dhal is thick and the lentils are cooked.

4 Remove from the heat and stir in the coriander and kale. Allow to cool completely, then portion into containers and freeze. Defrost in the fridge overnight and reheat in the microwave until piping hot. Serve with coriander and a sprinkling of pumpkin seeds.

CHEESY MUSHROOM & THYME SCONES

YOU COULD MAKE THESE SCONES IN A FOOD PROCESSOR, ALTHOUGH A COUPLE OF EXTRA MINUTES OF THERAPEUTICALLY PREPARING THEM BY HAND WILL MAKE FOR A MUCH LIGHTER AND WONDERFULLY CRUMBLY RESULT.

VEGETARIAN | MAKES 8

115 g (4 oz/scant ½ cup) chilled
  unsalted butter, cut into small cubes
200 g (7 oz/2¼ cups) button
  mushrooms, finely sliced
2 garlic cloves, minced
10 sprigs of thyme, leaves only
2 heaped tbsp roughly chopped chives
2 pinches salt
400 g (14 oz/3¼ cups) plain
  (all-purpose) flour
3 tsp baking powder
75 g (2¾ oz/¾ cup) Parmesan, grated
  plus extra for topping
210 ml (7 fl oz) semi-skinned milk
1 large egg, lightly beaten
ricotta, to serve (optional)
caramelised onions (page 32, step 2),
  to serve
butter, to serve (optional)

1 Preheat the oven to 180°C (350°F/ Gas 4) and line a baking tray with baking parchment.

2 In a medium saucepan, melt 1 tablespoon of the butter over a low heat, then add the mushrooms, garlic, thyme and chives. Season with a pinch of salt and sauté until the mushrooms are tender, around 8–10 minutes. Set aside.

3 In a large bowl, sift in the flour, baking powder and a pinch of salt. Add the remaining butter and, using your fingertips, rub the butter into the flour until the mixture resembles coarse breadcrumbs. Gently stir in the Parmesan and mushrooms.

4 Using a blunt butter knife or pastry blender (this maintains the flaky texture), cut the milk into the flour and butter mixture to form a dough. It may seem a bit dry, but it will come together eventually.

5 Turn the dough out onto a clean worksurface and knead twice or until smooth. Shape into a 17 cm (7 in) round, cut into 8 wedges and place on the lined baking tray.

6 Brush the egg over the scones, sprinkle over extra Parmesan and bake in the oven for 20–25 minutes or until risen and golden brown. Transfer to a wire rack to cool.

7 Wrap tightly in cling film (plastic wrap) and freeze in a container.

8 When ready to eat, defrost in the fridge overnight and reheat in the microwave until heated through. Halve and serve with ricotta and caramelised onions, or a humble swipe of butter.

ROAST LEEK, PEA & MINT SOUP

*THIS IS SPRING IN A SOUP.
THE CARAMELISED ROAST LEEKS
ADDS A SUBTLE SWEETNESS,
MADE PERFECTLY CREAMY FROM
THE CRÈME FRAÎCHE.*

**VEGETARIAN | GLUTEN-FREE
MAKES 4–5 BOWLS**

4 large leeks, cut into small chunks
90 ml (3 fl oz) olive oil
1 large brown onion, roughly diced
2 garlic cloves, roughly chopped
400 g (14 oz/generous 3 cups) frozen
 peas
1 litre (34 fl oz) vegetable stock
1 ripe avocado, peeled and stoned
1 tbsp crème fraîche
½ small bunch of mint, plus extra
 to garnish
juice of ½ lemon, plus extra to taste
salt and freshly ground black pepper
feta, to garnish

1 Preheat the oven to 200°C (400°F/ Gas 6). Line a roasting tray with baking parchment. Lay the leeks on the tray, cut side up. Drizzle over 60 ml (2 fl oz) of the olive oil, and sprinkle a generous pinch of salt on top. Roast the leeks in the oven for 15 minutes or until tender and caramelised.

2 Heat the remaining oil in a large saucepan, add the onion and sauté for 2 minutes until soft and translucent. Add the garlic, cook for 1 minute, then add the frozen peas and roasted leeks and pour over the stock.

3 Bring the mixture to the boil, then reduce to a simmer for 5 minutes or until the peas have defrosted.

4 Remove the pan from the heat. Add the avocado, crème fraîche, mint and lemon juice and blitz with a hand blender until smooth. Add extra lemon juice if needed, and season to taste. Once cooked, remove from the heat and allow to cool completely.

5 Portion the soup into containers and freeze. Defrost in the fridge overnight, and reheat in the microwave until heated through. Serve with a sprinkle of feta and mint and more seasoning, if required.

COURGETTE & RICOTTA LASAGNE

THIS IS A FRESH TAKE ON THE CLASSIC LASGANE. MADE WITH A GENEROUS PORTION OF HERBS, AND COURGETTE LAYERS TO REPLACE PASTA, YOU'LL BE FEELING LIGHT AND ZIPPY WITH THIS WARM WEATHER ALTERNATIVE.

VEGETARIAN | GLUTEN-FREE
MAKES 4–6 LUNCH PORTIONS

olive oil, for greasing
1 large broccoli crown, cut into florets,
   then sliced lengthways
300 g (10½ oz/6 cups) spinach
600 g (1 lb 5 oz/scant 2½ cups) ricotta
2 garlic cloves, minced
½ small bunch of basil, leaves only,
   roughly chopped
½ small bunch of flat-leaf parsley,
   leaves only, roughly chopped
½ small bunch of mint, leaves only,
   roughly chopped
850 g (1 lb 14 oz/3½ cups) passata
4 large courgettes (zucchini), peeled
   into ribbons
150 g (5¼ oz/1½ cups) Parmesan,
   grated
2 tbsp balsamic vinegar
salt and freshly ground black pepper

1 Preheat the oven to 200°C (400°F/ Gas 6). Grease a 23 cm (9 in) deep baking dish with olive oil.

2 Fill a small saucepan with salted water and bring to the boil. Add the broccoli, bring back to the boil and cook for 1–2 minutes or until just crisp and tender. Remove with a slotted spoon, and place in a bowl of ice-cold water.

3 In the same saucepan, fit in a steaming pot and fill with the spinach. Reduce to a simmer, cover and steam for 2 minutes until the spinach has wilted. Remove from the pan, and squeeze out as much water as possible.

4 In a large bowl, stir together the ricotta, garlic, basil, parsley and mint with a pinch of salt and pepper.

5 Spread one third of the passata over the base of the dish, top with half of the courgette ribbons, the spinach and broccoli, one-third of the ricotta mixture and one-third of the Parmesan. Repeat the layering once more. Drizzle over the balsamic vinegar and top with the remaining passata, ricotta and Parmesan.

6 Place the dish on a baking tray, (in case any sauce bubbles over) and bake for 20 minutes or until golden on top and bubbling. Set aside to cool completely.

7 Cut the lasagne into 4–6 portions, place each serving into containers and freeze. When ready to eat, defrost in the fridge overnight, and reheat in the microwave until piping hot.

CARAMELISED ONION, MUSHROOM & GOAT'S CHEESE FRITTATA

YOU CAN ALSO COOK YOUR FRITTATA IN INDIVIDUAL MUFFIN CASES TO MAKE QUICK-GRAB MEALS THAT WILL DEFROST IN TIME FOR LUNCH! SIMPLY POUR THE MIX INTO 10 MINI MUFFIN CASES AND BAKE FOR 12 MINUTES OR UNTIL LIGHTLY GOLDEN AND JUST SET.

VEGETARIAN | GLUTEN-FREE
MAKES 4–6 LUNCH PORTIONS

3 tbsp olive oil
300 g (10½ oz/3⅓ cups) mushrooms, sliced
small bunch of thyme (about 10 sprigs)
2 red onions, sliced into fine wedges
1 tbsp brown sugar
1 tbsp balsamic vinegar
9 large eggs
3 tbsp milk, semi-skimmed or whole (full-fat)
3 tbsp chopped dill, plus extra to garnish
100 g (3½ oz/⅔ cup) goat's cheese, crumbled
salt and freshly ground black pepper

1 Heat 1 tablespoon of the oil in a deep ovenproof saucepan (22 cm/ 8½ in) over a medium heat. Add the mushrooms and thyme and sauté until tender. Remove the mushrooms from the pan and set aside.

2 In the same saucepan, heat the remaining oil over a low heat. Add the onions and cook for 10 minutes or until softened and lightly golden, stirring regularly. Stir in the sugar and vinegar and cook for a further 5 minutes or until caramelised.

3 Preheat the oven to 200°C (400°F/ Gas 6). In a bowl, whisk together the eggs and milk, stir in the dill, mushrooms and half the goat's cheese, then season to taste. Pour this into the saucepan with the caramelised onions, making sure no onions are stuck to the bottom of the pan, stirring gently.

4 Cook the frittata mixture for 2 minutes or until the edges start to set. Sprinkle over the remaining goat's cheese and cook in the oven for 15 minutes or until golden and set. Allow to cool.

5 Cut the frittata into portions, wrap in cling film (plastic wrap), place in containers and freeze. When ready to eat, defrost in the fridge overnight, and reheat in the microwave until warm. Garnish with fresh dill, to serve.

POLENTA PIZZA BAKE

THE FIRST THING THAT CAME TO MIND WHEN EATING THIS WAS 'MARGHERITA PIZZA'. PACKED FULL OF VEGETABLES, IT'S THE PIZZA BUT NOT AS YOU KNOW IT.

VEGETARIAN | GLUTEN-FREE
MAKES 6 LUNCH PORTIONS

FOR THE RAGU
butter, for greasing
2–3 tbsp olive oil
2 garlic cloves, minced
2 aubergines (eggplants), cubed
1 courgette (zucchini), finely sliced
1 red (bell) pepper, cut into thin strips
350 g (12¼ oz/1½ cups) passata
2 tbsp balsamic vinegar
1 bunch of basil, roughly chopped
150 g (5¼ oz/1 cup) bocconcini (baby mozzarella), sliced
salt and freshly ground black pepper

FOR THE POLENTA
810 ml (27 fl oz) vegetable or chicken stock
200 g (7 oz/1⅓ cups) instant polenta
1 tbsp olive oil
1 tbsp dried oregano
100 g (3½ oz/1 cup) Parmesan, grated
100 g (3½ oz/2 cups) spinach, roughly chopped

1 Preheat the oven to 200°C (400°F/Gas 6). Grease a 20 × 30 cm (8 ×12 in) baking dish with butter.

2 Make the ragu by heating 2 tablespoons of the oil in a medium saucepan over a medium heat. Add the garlic, aubergine, courgette, and pepper. Cook for 10 minutes or until the vegetables have softened and shrunk, adding more oil if needed.

3 Pour the passata over the vegetables, stir through the balsamic vinegar and half the basil and leave to simmer for 10 minutes. Season to taste.

4 Meanwhile, for the polenta, bring the stock to the boil in a medium saucepan. While whisking, slowly pour the polenta into the pan. Over a moderate heat, whisk in the oil and oregano, and continue whisking for another 5 minutes or until thick. Stir in half the Parmesan and the spinach.

5 Pour the polenta into the dish, top with the ragu, bocconcini and the remaining basil and Parmesan. Bake for 15 minutes or until golden and heated through. Set aside to cool.

6 Cut the polenta bake into portions, place into containers and freeze. When ready to eat, defrost in the fridge overnight and reheat in the microwave until warmed through.

LENTIL & DUKKAH BALLS

*THIS RECIPE USES TINNED
LENTILS FOR SPEED, BUT OF
COURSE HOME-COOKED LENTILS
WOULD BE PERFECT, TOO. ENJOY
ON ITS OWN, OR FOR EXTRA
SUBSTANCE, EAT WITH PASTA,
COUSCOUS OR ANY GRAIN
OF CHOICE.*

VEGETARIAN | DAIRY-FREE
MAKES 3–4 LUNCH PORTIONS

FOR THE MEATBALLS

1 tbsp olive oil, plus extra for brushing
1 red onion, diced
2 garlic cloves, chopped
2 courgettes (zucchini), grated
2 × 400 g (14 oz) tins green lentils,
  drained and rinsed
30 g (1 oz/scant ¼ cup) cashews
30 g (1 oz/scant ¼ cup) almonds
3 tbsp chopped mint leaves
3 heaped tbsp dukkah
1 tsp ground cumin
½ tsp chilli flakes
zest of 1 lemon
juice of 2 lemons
2 slices of bread, blitzed into breadcrumbs (for gluten-free, use any
  gluten-free bread substitute)
1 large egg

FOR THE SAUCE

1 tbsp olive oil
1 tbsp cumin seeds
1 tsp chilli flakes
1 garlic clove, minced
200 g (7 oz) tin chickpeas (garbanzo
  beans), rinsed and drained
1 red (bell) pepper, sliced lengthways
400 g (14 oz) tin tomatoes
250 g (8¾ oz/1 cup) passata
3 tbsp roughly chopped mint
4 tbsp roughly chopped parsley

TO SERVE

pasta or grain of choice

1 Preheat the oven to 200°C (400°F/
Gas 6). Heat the oil in a small
saucepan over a medium heat, add
the onions and sauté until soft. Add
the garlic and courgettes and cook
for a further 5 minutes, until the
courgettes have softened.

2 In a food processor, combine the
lentils with the rest of the ingredients.
Blitz in bursts until the mixture holds
firmly together.

3 Shape the lentil mixture into 18 balls
(around 1 heaped tablespoon each),
place on a tray, brush with oil and bake
in the oven for 20 minutes or until
golden and crisp.

(CONTINUED OVERLEAF)

4 Meanwhile, make the sauce by heating the oil in a medium saucepan, add the cumin seeds, chilli flakes and garlic, and fry for 2 minutes. Add the chickpeas and red pepper, followed by the tomatoes, passata, mint and parsley. Simmer for 10 minutes, then gently toss through the meatballs. Once cooked, take off the heat and allow to cool completely.

5 Portion into containers and freeze. When ready to heat, defrost in the fridge overnight and reheat in the microwave until warmed through. Serve by itself or alongside your grain of choice.

RAS EL HANOUT QUINOA BURGERS

THIS LIGHTER VERSION OF A BURGER IS FILLED WITH CHICKPEAS, QUINOA AND PLENTY OF SPICES TO PIMP UP YOUR WEEKDAY LUNCH. ASSEMBLE YOUR BURGER AT YOUR DESK OR BULK IT OUT WITH A SALAD.

VEGETARIAN | DAIRY-FREE | MAKES 10 LUNCH PORTIONS

185 g (6½ oz/scant 1 cup) quinoa
500 ml (17 fl oz) vegetable stock
2 tsp cumin seeds
3 tbsp olive oil
4 spring onions (scallions), sliced
2 garlic cloves, minced
200 g (7 oz) tin chickpeas (garbanzo beans), rinsed and drained
155 g (5½ oz/generous 1¼ cups) frozen peas
2 tbsp ras el hanout paste
2 large eggs, beaten
juice of 1 lemon
90 g (3¼ oz/¾ cup) plain (all-purpose) flour or gluten-free alternative
1 tbsp sesame seeds, plus extra to sprinkle
salt and freshly ground black pepper

TO SERVE

bread rolls, pita or bread of choice
hummus (page 89)
sliced tomatoes
chopped parsley

1 In a small saucepan, bring the quinoa and stock to the boil, then reduce to a simmer. Cook for 15 minutes or until the stock is absorbed and the quinoa is tender. Set aside.

2 Heat a medium saucepan over a high heat and toast the cumin seeds for around 1 minute until golden in colour and aromatic. Remove from the pan and set aside.

3 Heat 1 tablespoon of the oil in the same saucepan, add the spring onions and garlic and cook for 2 minutes to soften the onions. Add the chickpeas and peas and stir until the peas have defrosted. Spoon in the ras el hanout then remove the pan from the heat.

4 In a bowl, combine the cooked quinoa, toasted cumin seeds, chickpea mixture, eggs, lemon juice, flour, sesame seeds and season to taste.

5 Shape the mixture into 10 equal-sized patties. Heat the remaining 2 tablespoons of oil in a large non-stick frying pan (skillet) over a high heat. Cook the patties in batches for around 5 minutes on each side until golden and crispy, adding more oil if needed. Drain the patties on kitchen paper.

6 When completely cool, wrap the individual patties in cling film (plastic wrap), place in airtight containers, label and freeze. When ready to eat, defrost in the fridge overnight and reheat in the microwave until heated through. Serve in rolls or pita, with hummus, tomato slices and parsley.

For lunch that requires a little more preparation, but is happy to sit in the fridge overnight. You could make these meals for dinner, then pack the leftovers away for lunch the next day, because you already know how good they're going to be.

THE NIGHT BEFORE

3

MISO SALMON PARCELS WITH ASIAN NOODLES

BAKING THE SALMON ALL IN ONE UNIFIES YOUR WHOLE MEAL IN AN EASY-TO-TRANSPORT PARCEL.

GLUTEN-FREE | DAIRY-FREE
MAKES 2 LUNCH PORTIONS

85 g (3 oz/¾ cup) vermicelli noodles
2 tbsp sesame oil
2 garlic cloves, finely sliced
1 red chilli, deseeded and finely sliced
3 pak choi (bok choy), chopped into
 stems and leaves
100 g (3½ oz) green beans
3 tbsp soy sauce
juice of 1 lime
3 spring onions (scallions), sliced
3 tbsp roughly chopped coriander
 (cilantro) leaves
2 tbsp white miso paste
1 tbsp mirin
1 tbsp grated fresh root ginger
2 × 140 g (5 oz) salmon fillets
2 tsp sesame seeds

TO SERVE
1 avocado, peeled, stoned and sliced
½ bunch of watercress
lime wedges

1 Preheat the oven to 200°C (400°F/ Gas 6). Cover the vermicelli in boiling water and leave for 5 minutes, then drain, rinse and set aside.

2 Heat the sesame oil in a medium saucepan and fry the garlic and chilli for 1 minute. Add the pak choi stems, green beans, soy sauce and lime juice, toss to coat and cook for 2 minutes. Remove from the heat, add the pak choi leaves then toss through the vermicelli, 2 tablespoons of the spring onions and 2 tablespoons of the coriander leaves.

3 In a small bowl, mix together the miso paste, mirin and ginger, and evenly brush the sauce over each of the salmon fillets.

4 Divide the noodles between 2 large squares of baking parchment on an oven tray and place the salmon fillets on top. Sprinkle over the sesame seeds, and the remaining spring onions and coriander leaves. Fold the paper up and twist to seal. Cook in the oven for 12–15 minutes until the fish flakes easily when tested with a fork. Once cooked, allow it to cool.

5 Pack the miso salmon parcels into lunch boxes and store in the fridge overnight. Serve with the avocado, watercress and lime wedges.

STUFFED AUBERGINES

COUSCOUS IS THE ULTIMATE QUICK-AND-EASY GRAIN, PERFECT FOR THIS MIDDLE EASTERN-INSPIRED LUNCH.

VEGETARIAN
MAKES 4 LUNCH PORTIONS

2 medium aubergines (eggplants)
90 ml (3 fl oz) olive oil
1 tbsp ground cumin
½ tsp cayenne pepper
150 g (5 oz/generous ¾ cup)
    couscous
210 ml (7 fl oz) boiling water
1 garlic clove, minced
2 heaped tbsp finely chopped mint
    leaves
2 heaped tbsp roughly chopped
    coriander (cilantro)
3 spring onions (scallions), sliced
50 g (1¾ oz/⅓ cup) pistachios,
    roughly chopped, plus extra to
    garnish
juice of 1 lime, plus extra to serve
100 g (3½ oz/⅔ cup) feta, crumbled
85 g (3 oz/⅔ cup) pomegranate seeds
salt and freshly ground black pepper

(CONTINUED OVERLEAF)

1 Preheat the oven to 200°C (400°F/ Gas 6). Line a baking tray with baking parchment.

2 Cut the aubergines in half, and using a small knife, gently cut a 1 cm (½ in) border inside each half. Scoop out the flesh inside the border and set aside for later. Place the aubergine halves on the lined baking tray, brush the inside with 2 tablespoons of the oil. Sprinkle over the ground cumin and cayenne pepper. Cover with foil and roast for 10 minutes or until just tender.

3 In a small bowl, combine the couscous with the boiling water and a pinch of salt. Stir to combine, cover and set aside for 8 minutes, or until the liquid is fully absorbed. Fluff with a fork, and stir through 1 tablespoon of the oil.

4 Chop the reserved aubergine flesh into small pieces. Heat 2 tablespoons of the oil in a medium saucepan over a medium heat, then add the garlic, aubergine flesh and a pinch of salt. Sauté until soft.

5 Toss to combine the couscous, aubergine flesh, mint, coriander, spring onions, pistachios, lime juice and the remaining olive oil. Season to taste. Remove the foil from the baked aubergine halves, and fill with the couscous mixture. Bake for a further 10–15 minutes in the oven, or until lightly golden on top. Once cooked, allow to cool.

6 Pack the aubergines into lunch boxes and store in the fridge overnight, alongside the feta, pomegranate and extra lime juice to garnish. This is best served at room temperature.

SPEEDY RICOTTA & ROCKET GNOCCHI WITH HERB PESTO

A SIMPLE MIX AND FRY METHOD THAT WELCOMES THE RUSTIC COOK IN ALL OF US.

VEGETARIAN | MAKES 2 LUNCH PORTIONS

FOR THE PESTO

1 bunch of fresh basil
1 bunch of fresh mint
2 tbsp whole almonds, plus extra
    to garnish
4 tbsp grated Parmesan
2 small garlic cloves
juice of 1 lemon
210 ml (7 fl oz) olive oil
salt and freshly ground black pepper

FOR THE GNOCCHI

70 g (2½ oz/1½ cups) rocket
    (arugula), roughly chopped
250 g (8¾ oz/1 cup) ricotta
5 tbsp grated Parmesan, plus extra to
    garnish
1 large egg yolk
zest of 1 lemon
100 g (3½ oz/generous ¾ cup) plain
    (all-purpose) flour
80 ml (2½ fl oz) olive oil, plus extra
    for frying
salt and freshly ground black pepper

1 Make the pesto by blitzing all the ingredients in a food processor until everything is thoroughly combined. Season to taste. Pour into a small bowl and set aside.

2 To make the gnocchi, mix together the rocket, ricotta, Parmesan, egg yolk, lemon zest, flour and 2 tablespoons of the olive oil. Stir to form a thick dough and season to taste.

3 Heat a large frying pan (skillet) over a high heat with the remaining oil, and drop a large tablespoon of the gnocchi mixture into the pan. Cook for 2 minutes either side or until golden, crispy and firm to touch. Continue this process in batches until all the gnocchi is cooked, adding more oil to the pan if necessary, and draining the cooked gnocchi on paper towel.

4 Toss the gnocchi in the pesto and portion into lunch boxes. When ready to eat, reheat the gnocchi in a microwave until heated through and serve with almonds and Parmesan.

STUFFED PORTOBELLO MUSHROOMS

PORTOBELLO MUSHROOMS HAVE A STRONG, EARTHY FLAVOUR AND WILL FILL YOUR KITCHEN WITH A TANTILISING AROMA, MAKING THESE HARD TO SAVE FOR THE NEXT DAY.

VEGETARIAN | MAKES 4 LUNCH PORTIONS

4 large Portobello mushrooms
4 tbsp olive oil
30 g (1 oz/⅛ cup) butter
2 sprigs of rosemary
1 large red onion, cut into fine wedges
2 garlic cloves, minced
100 g (3½ oz/1⅔ cups) sun-dried
    tomatoes in oil, drained and halved,
    plus 2 tbsp of the oil
65 g (2¼ oz) sourdough bread, blitzed
    into breadcrumbs
1 tbsp pine nuts
1 tbsp dried oregano
120 g (4¼ oz/generous ¾ cup)
    mozzarella, cut into small pieces
50 g (1¾ oz/scant ½ cup) Cheddar,
    grated
salt and freshly ground black pepper

TO SERVE
salad leaves
balsamic dressing (optional)

1 Preheat the oven to 180°C (350°F/ Gas 4). Line a baking tray with baking parchment. Remove and reserve the stalks from the mushrooms and place the mushrooms on the tray. Drizzle 2 tablespoons of the oil over the mushrooms, place one-quarter of the butter on top of each, sprinkle over the rosemary leaves and season. Roast for 10 minutes. Remove from the oven and allow to cool.

2 Heat the remaining olive oil in a saucepan over a medium heat. Add the onion and sauté for 5 minutes, then add the garlic, mushroom stalks, sun-dried tomatoes and oil, and cook until soft.

4 Add the breadcrumbs, pine nuts and oregano. Increase the heat to high and cook until golden and crispy. Season.

5 Preheat the grill (broiler) to 200°C (400°F). Toss the mozzarella and Cheddar into the breadcrumb mixture and spoon in the mushroom cups. Grill (broil) until golden brown on top.

6 Once cooled, pack the mushrooms into a lunch box and store in the fridge. To serve, heat in a microwave until warmed through. Serve with the salad leaves and balsamic dressing.

ROASTED HARISSA CAULIFLOWER 'STEAK'

TRANSFORMING THE CAULIFLOWER, INTO A THICKLY SLICED 'STEAK' MAKES IT LIGHTER THAN YOUR USUAL MEAT HIT.

VEGETARIAN | VEGAN | DAIRY-FREE
MAKES 5 LUNCH PORTIONS

1 large cauliflower
3 tbsp harissa paste
zest and juice of 2 lemons
90 ml (3 fl oz) olive oil
150 g (5 oz/generous ¾ cup)
   wholewheat or white pearl couscous
200 g (7 oz) tin chickpeas (garbanzo
   beans), drained and rinsed
3 tbsp chopped parsley, plus extra
   to garnish
3 tbsp chopped coriander (cilantro),
   plus extra to garnish
50 g (1¾ oz/scant ½ cup) sultanas
   (golden raisins)
40 g (1½ oz/½ cup) flaked almonds,
   toasted
2 spring onions (scallions), finely sliced
salt and freshly ground black pepper

FOR THE DRESSING
juice of 1 lemon
1 tsp ground cumin
3 tbsp extra virgin olive oil

1 Preheat the oven to 200°C (400°F/Gas 6). Line a roasting tray with baking parchment.

2 Remove the leaves of the cauliflower, and trim the stem, leaving the core intact. Place the cauliflower on a chopping board and cut it into 5 thick slices, the 3 middle slices should remain intact, and the florets may fall away in the other slices. Lay all the cauliflower slices and florets on the lined roasting tray.

3 In a bowl, stir together the harissa, lemon zest, juice and olive oil. Spread the mixture all over the cauliflower slices and season. Roast for 25–30 minutes, turning halfway, until deep golden brown and caramelised.

4 To make the couscous, bring a small saucepan of salted water to the boil. Stir in the couscous, cover, and simmer until soft and cooked. Drain, rinse and set aside.

5 Make the dressing by whisking together all the ingredients. Season. Combine the couscous, chickpeas, parsley, coriander, sultanas, toasted almonds and spring onions with the dressing and stir well.

7 Portion the couscous into 5 lunch boxes, and top each with a cauliflower 'steak'. Store in the fridge overnight. Serve at room temperature.

SWEET POTATO, BULGUR WHEAT & CAULIFLOWER RICE SALAD

BY BLITZING THE CAULIFLOWER IN A FOOD PROCESSOR, YOU CREATE A FLUFFY, RICE-LIKE TEXTURE THAT COOKS IN HALF THE TIME — THE PERFECT SUBSTITUTE!

VEGETARIAN | VEGAN | GLUTEN-FREE | DAIRY-FREE | MAKES 4 LUNCH PORTIONS

4 medium sweet potatoes, cut into
  thin wedges
2 red onions, cut into wedges
2 tsp smoked paprika
90 ml (3 fl oz) olive oil
130 g (4½ oz/¾ cup) bulgur wheat
1 garlic clove, minced
1 cauliflower, blitzed
125 g (4 oz/3 cups) kale, chopped
2 avocados, peeled, stoned and diced
½ bunch of parsley, roughly chopped
salt and freshly ground black pepper
3 tbsp mixed seeds, to serve

FOR THE DRESSING
juice of 2 lemons
1 tbsp clear honey
½ tbsp wholegrain mustard
100 ml (3½ fl oz) olive oil
salt and freshly ground black pepper

1 Preheat the oven to 220°C (425°F/ Gas 7). Line a baking tray with baking parchment.

2 Toss the sweet potatoes and onions in the paprika with 5 tablespoons of the oil. Season well and place on the tray. Roast in the oven for 20 minutes until caramelised, stirring halfway through.

3 Pour the bulgur wheat into a small saucepan and cover with cold water. Bring to the boil, then simmer for 8–10 minutes or until tender. Drain, rinse and set aside.

4 Heat a medium saucepan over a medium heat with the remaining olive oil, add the garlic and cook for 1 minute, then add the cauliflower rice and stir in the pan until lightly golden. Add the kale and cook for a further minute until bright green.

5 Make the dressing by whisking together all the ingredients. Season to taste.

6 Arrange the salad by tossing together the roasted vegetables, bulgur wheat, cauliflower and kale mixture, avocados and parsley. Pack into lunch boxes, with the dressing in a separate container, and store in the fridge overnight. Serve at room temperature with a sprinkling of seeds.

CHEESY CAULIFLOWER & ARTICHOKE BAKE

A LIGHTER ALTERNATIVE TO THE CLASSIC CHEESY CAULIFLOWER, WITH ZERO COMPROMISE ON FLAVOUR.

VEGETARIAN | MAKES 2–3 LUNCH PORTIONS

500 ml (17 fl oz) vegetable stock
   or water
1 large cauliflower, trimmed and leaves
   removed
500 ml (17 fl oz) whole (full-fat) milk
2 garlic cloves
zest of 1 lemon
5 sprigs of thyme, leaves only
4 tbsp cornflour (cornstarch)
1 tsp Dijon mustard
pinch of nutmeg
80 g (3 oz/⅔ cup) Cheddar, grated
50 g (1¾ oz/½ cup) Parmesan, grated
150 g (5 oz/scant ⅔ cup) ricotta
100 g (3½ oz/1⅓ cups) Swiss chard,
   roughly chopped
200 g (7 oz/3⅓ cups) Globe artichoke
   hearts in oil, drained
2 slices of stale bread, blitzed into
   chunky breadcrumbs
2 tbsp olive oil
65 g (2 oz/generous ½ cup) walnuts
salt and freshly ground black pepper

1 Preheat the oven to 200°C (400°F/ Gas 6). Pour the stock or water into a medium pan and bring to the boil. Cut the cauliflower into small florets and add to the pan. Boil for 4 minutes or until just tender. Remove the cauliflower and discard the liquid.

2 In a small saucepan, bring the milk, garlic, lemon zest and thyme to a soft boil. Remove the garlic cloves, then whisk in the cornflour until the milk thickens and smooths. Add the mustard, nutmeg and cheeses and whisk to combine. Remove from the heat. Season to taste.

4 Pour a third of the cheese sauce into a 16 × 22 cm (6 × 8½ in) baking dish. Top with half the Swiss chard, half the artichoke hearts and half the cauliflower, then pour over another third of the cheese sauce. Repeat the vegetable layers, then top with the remaining cheese sauce. Sprinkle over the breadcrumbs and walnuts, then drizzle over the olive oil.

5 Bake in the oven for 15 minutes or until the cheese is bubbling and the top is golden brown. Sprinkle the walnuts on top just before the bake is ready. Once out of the oven, set aside to cool.

6 Cut the bake into portion sizes, place into lunch boxes, and leave in the fridge overnight. To serve, heat in the microwave until warmed through.

MINI CAPRESE CAULIFLOWER PIZZA

THIS GLUTEN-FREE ALTERNATIVE MEANS IT'S 100 PER CENT ACCEPTABLE TO HAVE PIZZA FOR LUNCH ANY DAY OF THE WEEK.

VEGETARIAN | GLUTEN-FREE
MAKES 2 LUNCH PORTIONS

1 large cauliflower
1 large egg
100 g (3½ oz/1 cup) ground almonds
3 tbsp grated Parmesan
2 heaped tbsp pesto (page 49)
250 g (8¾ oz/1⅔ cup) mozzarella,
   sliced
3 small tomatoes, sliced
basil leaves, to garnish

1 Preheat the oven to 180°C (350°F/ Gas 4). Line a baking tray with baking parchment.

2 Blitz the cauliflower in a food processor until it resembles fine breadcrumbs. Place the cauliflower in a microwave-proof dish and microwave on high for 5 minutes or until softened. Lay out a clean tea towel, and once the cauliflower is cool enough to handle, tip it onto the towel, wrap the sides up, and squeeze out as much moisture as you can. This will stop the pizza from becoming soggy.

3 In a bowl, combine the cooked cauliflower, egg, almonds and Parmesan. Stir well, then tip onto the tray and use your hands or a spoon to spread the cauliflower base into two circles, 25 cm (9 in) each. Make the edges slightly thicker to create a crust. Bake in the oven for 10–15 minutes or until golden brown. Set aside to cool.

4 Increase the oven temperature to 200°C (400°F/Gas 6). Spread the pesto over the pizza base, then arrange the mozzarella and tomato slices on top. Bake in the oven for 10 minutes or until the mozzarella has melted. Once cooked, set aside to cool.

5 Place the pizzas into 2 large lunch boxes (cut the pizzas into slices if need be), and store in the fridge overnight. To serve, heat the pizza in the microwave until warmed, and sprinkle over basil to garnish.

Combining ease with speed and of course, tons of flavour. These lunches can be thrown together in the morning, toothbrush in mouth and bed hair included. The recipes in this chapter are to act as a guideline and source of inspiration so you can adapt them to suit the ingredients you have in your kitchen.

4

IN THE MORNING

LUNCH IN A JAR

*NOT ONLY IS THIS WAY OF
PRESENTING YOUR LUNCH EASY
ON THE EYE, THE PRACTICALITY
OF THE PACKAGING VERGES ON
GENIUS. BRING YOUR SALAD TO
WORK WITHOUT THE DREAD OF
A SOGGY MESS. MOST MEALS CAN
LAST UP TO A WORKING WEEK IN
THE FRIDGE. SIMPLY TIP THE
CONTENTS OF YOUR JAR INTO
A BOWL AND LUNCH IS THERE,
READY TO GO.*

Successfully creating an 'all-in-one'
lunch jar comes down to the simple art
of layering. Once you have the method
figured out, you can go to town with
your own personalised meal.

TYPE OF JAR
Use a 1 litre (34 fl oz) jar per serving
or a 500 ml (17fl oz) jar if having as a
side. They need to be wide-mouthed
with tight-fitting lids (preserving jars
work best) – the tighter the seal, the
longer your greens stay crisp.

HOW TO ASSEMBLE
The key rules to transporting any
lunch jar is to place wet ingredients at
the bottom and ingredients that need
to stay dry at the top.

1 Always start with dressings at the
base, using however much you like.

2 Next, top with non-absorbent hard
vegetables such as carrot, cucumber,
chickpeas (garbanzo beans), onion,
beetroot (beets) and (bell) peppers.
This is a barrier layer that will help
make sure your greens won't go soggy.

3 As an extra layer of protection, top
with softer vegetables or fruit, such as
tomatoes, avocado (with a squeeze of
lemon to keep it green), mushrooms
and strawberries.

4 Now top with grains or pasta – this
can be anything from quinoa to
buckwheat, bulgur wheat, pasta
or noodles.

5 Next add the protein, such as egg,
chicken, tuna, meat, or cheeses like
feta and Parmesan. Meats should be
added on the day of eating if you're
making the salad ahead of time.

6 Crunch time. Literally. Seeds, nuts
and dried fruit are sprinkled on top.

7 The crisp, leafy greens are last to
go on, perhaps even with a generous
serving of herbs.

8 Seal tightly and store in the fridge
until ready to eat.

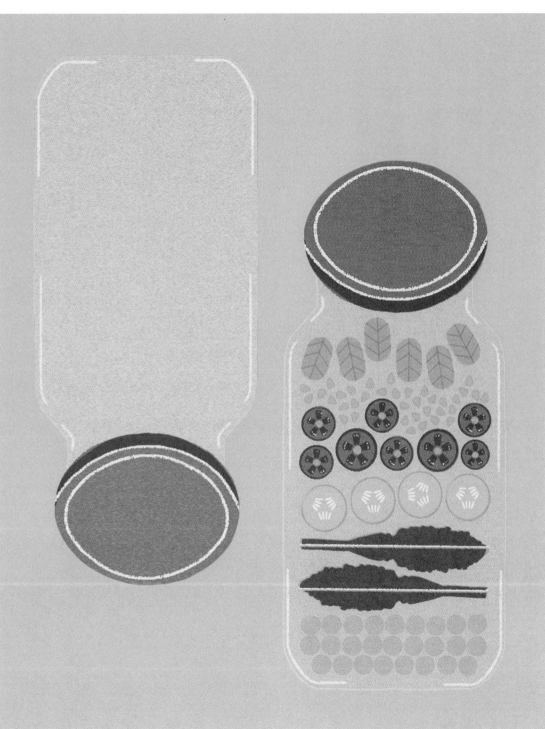

BALSAMIC, POMEGRANATE & ROCKET JAR SALAD

THIS HAS ALL THE ELEMENTS A SALAD SHOULD: ACIDITY, CRUNCH, FRESHNESS, BITE AND SUSTAINING POWER SO IT CAN STAND ALONE AS A MEAL. IT CAN ALSO LAST UP TO THREE DAYS IN THE FRIDGE AS AN ADDED BONUS.

VEGETARIAN | MAKES 1 LUNCH PORTION
FILLS 1 × 1 LITRE (34 FL OZ) JAR

1 tbsp balsamic vinegar
3 tbsp olive oil
50 g (1¾ oz/scant ½ cup) green beans
¼ small red onion, sliced
½ avocado, peeled, stoned and cubed
½ pear, finely sliced
1 tsp lemon juice
3 tsp pomegranate seeds
70 g (2½ oz/generous ⅓ cup) cooked
  freekeh
small handful of Parmesan shavings
4 tbsp walnuts, halved
small handful of watercress
small handful of rocket (arugula)
salt and freshly ground black pepper

1 Dressing: pour the balsamic and olive oil into the bottom of the jar and swirl to combine, then sprinkle in the seasoning.

2 Hard vegetables: blanch the green beans by bringing a small pot of salted water to the boil and cooking for 2 minutes or until bright green, then immediately remove and shock in ice cold water (this can be done the night before). Add the green beans and onion to the jar.

3 Soft fruit: add the avocado and pear, with lemon juice on top to prevent both going brown. Then add the pomegranate seeds.

4 Grains: spoon in the freekeh.

5 Protein: sprinkle over the Parmesan.

6 Crunch: add the walnuts.

7 Leafy greens: pack in the watercress and rocket.

8 Seal: tighten the lid, and store in the fridge. Tip into a bowl to serve.

THAI GREEN COCONUT CURRY INSTANT JAR SOUP

THE ULTIMATE QUICK SOUP. SIMPLY POUR HOT WATER OVER TO SERVE AND YOU'RE GOOD TO GO! NATURALLY, ACCESS TO A KETTLE IS AN ESSENTIAL FOR THIS LUNCH.

VEGETARIAN | VEGAN | GLUTEN-FREE | DAIRY-FREE | MAKES 1 LUNCH SERVING FILLS 1 X 1 LITRE (34 FL OZ) JAR

½–1 tbsp Thai green curry paste, according to taste
3 tbsp coconut milk
3 tsp soy sauce
1 tsp bouillon powder (or ½ stock cube)
½ pak choi (bok choy), cut into wedges
40 g (1½ oz/⅓ cup) mangetout (snow peas)
1 carrot, peeled into ribbons
30 g (1 oz/¼ cup) vermicelli rice noodles
1 heaped tbsp chopped coriander (cilantro)
1 spring onion (scallion), finely sliced
½ lime
boiling water, to serve

1 Dressing: spoon the Thai green curry paste, coconut milk, soy sauce and stock powder into the jar and stir to combine.

2 Hard vegetables: place the pak choi on top.

3 Soft vegetables: add the mangetout and carrot ribbons.

4 Grains: add the vermicelli on top.

5 Leafy greens: sprinkle over the coriander, spring onion and place the lime on top.

6 Seal: tighten the lid, and store in the fridge. When ready to serve, remove the lime wedge and pour over enough boiling water to cover all the ingredients, then put the lid back on and leave to sit for 2 minutes. Stir to combine or tip into a bowl. Squeeze over the lime and enjoy.

HOMEMADE
BENTO BOX

THIS IS LUNCH IN ITS RAWEST FORM, TAKING US BACK TO ITS JAPANESE ROOTS, WHERE THE ART OF COMPARTMENTALISATION WAS MASTERED LONG BEFORE THE LUNCH BOX GRACED OUR SCHOOLBAGS.

Bento boxes don't have a specific list of ingredients or quantities that they need to contain, leaving it open to the interpretations of you and your fridge. Here are some basic ingredient categories to help you get the most out of your bento box.

GRAINS AND PULSES: A chance to use up any leftover grains or get creative and cook some to suit the flavour combination you're aiming for. Options include: wild rice, quinoa, bulgur wheat, buckwheat, farro, pearl barley, spelt, soba noodles, lentils or millet.

VEGETABLES: These can be raw, cooked or a combination of both. Roasting a whole batch of vegetables and refrigerating them until needed is a great way to grab and go in the morning. This can include sweet potatoes, beetroot, squash, courgette and mushrooms.

Raw vegetables can range from radishes, carrot and cucumber to shelled edamame beans.

LEAFY GREENS: Another opportunity to be resourceful and scour the fridge. You can use anything – kale, rocket (arugula), spinach, Swiss chard, watercress, cabbage (red cabbage for more colour), lettuce or pak choi (bok choy)... the possibilities are endless.

PROTEIN: To make a more sustaining lunch, add protein such as smoked salmon, tofu, egg, chickpeas (garbanzo beans), chicken or cheese.

DRESSING AND ACIDIC HIT: Add an extra zing with tahini, lemon juice, kimchi, pickled ginger, lime, miso dressing, herb yoghurt or sauerkraut.

GOOD FATS: Bring some balance with avocado, nuts, seeds, chia, coconut oil, and nut butters.

EXTRA FLAVOUR AND TEXTURE: Time to garnish up a storm. Fresh herbs, spices, soy sauce, are all at your disposal.

SUSHI BOWL BENTO

SAVE TIME ON INDIVIDUALLY ROLLING YOUR SUSHI BY HAND AND PUT EVERYTHING YOU LOVE ABOUT IT INTO ONE BOX.

GLUTEN-FREE | DAIRY-FREE

Grain: rice (brown, white or wild)
Vegetables: cucumber, sliced radishes, edamame beans, carrot, sesame seeds
Leafy greens: kale
Protein: smoked salmon
Dressing and acidic hits: pickled ginger, lime juice
Healthy fats: sliced avocado, black sesame seeds
Extra flavour and texture: nori sheets, soy sauce, coriander (cilantro)

(IMAGE ON PREVIOUS PAGE)

BUDDHA BOWL BENTO

THIS RECIPE IS ALL ABOUT CELEBRATING PLANT-BASED FOODS, AND IS USUALLY ENJOYED IN A DEEP ROUND BOWL SO IT HAS A FULL ROUND BELLY, LIKE BUDDHA HIMSELF.

VEGAN | VEGETARIAN | DAIRY-FREE

Grain: spelt
Vegetables: roasted sweet potato, mushrooms
Leafy greens: cabbage, spinach
Protein: chickpeas (garbanzo beans), hummus
Dressing and acidic hits: lemon, honey and tahini dressing
Healthy fats: almonds
Extra flavour and texture: parsley, paprika

THE OPEN SANDWICH

THERE IS SO MUCH SIMPLE BEAUTY IN THE HUMBLE OPEN SANDWICH. YOU GET DOUBLE THE FILLING, FOR THE SAME AMOUNT OF BREAD AS A SANDWICH, PLUS IT CAN ALL BE EASILY ASSEMBLED JUST BEFORE EATING. THIS STYLE OF LUNCHING COULDN'T BE MORE AVAILABLE TO CREATIVE FREEDOM.

With lots of small bits and pieces to bring to and from work, this is the perfect opportunity to utilise your 'desk drawer' pantry and fill it will 'sandwich toppers' such as spices, nut butters and other garnishes, to avoid tedious ingredient transport.

BASIC COMPONENTS

BREAD

Blindingly obvious, but this is the true essence of your sandwich. Fluffy texture? Nutty and crunchy? So many options you could choose from depending on your mood. Choices can range from the classic sourdough, Danish rye bread, multigrain loaf, even gluten-free, if need be. Either way, good-quality bread will make all the difference.

SPREAD

A small detail that can sometimes be forgotten in the sandwich-making process, yet crucial in carrying the essence of the overall flavour. Choose from pesto, spiced or herby mayos, hummus, mashed avocado, nut butters or even a humble spread of butter to add a creamy flavour.

TOPPINGS

This is where you get to go wild. Make it as simple or as complex as you like – this is a chance for you to indulge in your favourite flavours. Get creative and play with textures.

GARNISH

Never underestimate the power of a garnish. Spruce with seeds, herbs, citrus juice, rocket (arugula), alfalfa, crumbled cheese or even a simple hint of cracked pepper makes a world of difference.

CLOCKWISE FROM TOP LEFT: AVOCADO WITH RADISH, FETA & DUKKAH; HUMMUS WITH ROAST PEPPERS & RED ONIONS; RICOTTA WITH MIXED TOMATOES & BASIL; BANANA WITH ALMOND BUTTER & CINNAMON

AVOCADO WITH RADISH, FETA & DUKKAH

THE AVOCADO IS ALWAYS SUCH A RELIABLE OPTION FOR LUNCH. TOPPED WITH A HINT OF DUKKAH AND CRISP RADISH TO ELEVATE THIS FAVOURITE.

VEGETARIAN | MAKES 1 LUNCH PORTION

2 slices of bread of choice
1 ripe avocado, peeled and stoned
1 tbsp dukkah
3 radishes, finely sliced
½ tbsp roughly chopped mint leaves
small handful of feta
juice of ½ lemon

1 To pack, fill a large lunch box with bread wrapped in cling film (plastic wrap), avocado, dukkah, radishes, mint and feta sealed in separate small bags, and half a lemon.

2 To assemble, spread the avocado over the bread, sprinkle over the dukkah. Arrange the radishes, mint and cheese on top and finish with a squeeze of lemon juice.

RICOTTA WITH MIXED TOMATOES & BASIL

RICOTTA IS SUCH A CREAMY AND DELICATE FLAVOURED CHEESE THAT IT MAKES IT THE PERFECT SPREAD TO ACCOMPANY SEASONALLY SWEET HEIRLOOM TOMATOES.

VEGETARIAN | MAKES 1 LUNCH PORTION

2 slices of bread of choice
2 large heirloom tomatoes, sliced
2 heaped tbsp ricotta
small handful of basil leaves
small handful of pine nuts, toasted
salt and freshly ground black pepper

1 To pack, fill a large lunch box with bread wrapped in cling film (plastic wrap), tomatoes, a small container filled with ricotta, and basil and pine nuts sealed in separate small bags.

2 To assemble, spread the ricotta over the bread and top with the tomatoes. Sprinkle the basil and pine nuts on top and season well.

BANANA WITH ALMOND BUTTER & CINNAMON

FOR THE LUNCHER THAT PREFERS THEIR MEALS ON THE SLIGHTLY SWEETER SIDE. YOU CAN USE WHICHEVER NUT BUTTER YOU HAVE AVAILABLE.

VEGETARIAN | VEGAN | DAIRY-FREE | MAKES 1 LUNCH PORTION

2 slices of bread of choice
2 tbsp almond butter
1 large banana, sliced
1 tsp cinnamon
1 tbsp coconut chips, toasted
honey, to drizzle

1 To pack, fill a large lunch box with bread wrapped in cling film (plastic wrap), a small container filled with almond butter, the banana, cinnamon and coconut chips sealed in separate small bags, and a small container of honey.

2 To assemble, spread the almond butter over the bread, top with the banana, then sprinkle over the cinnamon, coconut chips and drizzle on the honey.

HUMMUS WITH ROAST PEPPERS & RED ONIONS

THE SWEETNESS OF THE ONIONS AND PEPPERS COMPLEMENT THE CREAMY HUMMUS PERFECTLY. FOR SPEED, USE LEFTOVER ONIONS FROM YOUR LAST VEGGIE ROAST.

VEGETARIAN | VEGAN | DAIRY-FREE | MAKES 1 LUNCH PORTION

¼ red onion
a drizzle of olive oil
2 slices of bread of choice
2 heaped tbsp hummus
handful of rocket (arugula)
2 large handfuls of jarred (bell) peppers
½ tbsp chopped parsley
1 tbsp sunflower seeds

1 Preheat the oven to 220°C (425°F/ Gas 7). Coat the onion in the oil and roast for 5 minutes until caramelised.

2 To pack, fill a large lunch box with bread wrapped in cling film (plastic wrap), a small container filled with hummus, the rocket, red peppers, red onion, parsley and sunflower seeds sealed in separate small bags.

3 To assemble, spread the hummus over the bread, top with the rocket, peppers, onion, parsley and seeds.

COURGETTE RIBBONS WITH PEA & MINT SALAD

THE ULTIMATE SPEEDY SALAD, MAKING THE MOST OF FRESH AND ACCESSIBLE INGREDIENTS. RECOMMENDED ON THE HOTTEST OF SUMMER DAYS.

VEGETARIAN | GLUTEN-FREE
MAKES 1 LUNCH SERVING

handful of walnuts, toasted
1 courgette (zucchini), peeled into
　ribbons
30 g (1 oz/⅔ cup) rocket (arugula)
1 spring onion (scallion), sliced
50 g (1¾ oz/⅓ cup) fresh shelled peas
1 heaped tbsp roughly chopped mint
　leaves
30 g (1 oz/generous ¼ cup) feta

FOR THE DRESSING
juice of 1 lemon
½ tsp chilli flakes
2 tbsp olive oil
salt and freshly ground black pepper

1 In a small dry frying pan (skillet), over a low heat, toast the walnuts until aromatic, pour into a small bowl to cool. Toss together the courgette ribbons, rocket, spring onion, peas, mint leaves, walnuts and feta cheese. Place in a lunch box, and store in the fridge until needed.

2 To make the dressing, combine the lemon juice, chilli flakes, oil and seasoning in a small screw-top lidded jar and shake to combine.

3 To serve, pour the dressing over the salad, and toss to combine.

NO-BAKE MEDITERRANEAN FLATBREAD PIZZA

PIZZA THAT IS READY IN SECONDS IS ALWAYS A WIN. AIM FOR A GOOD-QUALITY PASSATA AND FLATBREAD FOR THE TASTIEST RESULTS.

VEGETARIAN | MAKES 1 LUNCH PORTION

1 large wholewheat flatbread
2 tbsp passata
1 tomato, sliced
½ red onion, finely sliced
handful of shaved Parmesan
handful of mozzarella, torn
100 g (3½ oz/¾ cup) mixed olives, pitted
handful of basil leaves
1 tsp dried oregano

1 To pack: fill a large lunch box with flatbread wrapped in cling film (plastic wrap), a small container filled with passata, and tomato, red onion, mozzerella, Parmesan, olives, basil and oregano sealed in separate small bags.

2 To assemble, spread the passata over the flatbread, then lay the tomato slices on top. Evenly sprinkle over the red onion, Parmesan, mozzarella, olives, basil leaves and oregano.

RADISH, KALE & FETA PITA POCKETS

NO NEED TO WORRY ABOUT SALAD FALLING OUT THE SIDES OF YOUR SANDWICH ANY MORE. THE PITA POCKET CONTAINS EVERYTHING IN ONE TIDY HANDFUL!

VEGETARIAN | MAKES 1 LUNCH PORTION

handful of finely sliced red cabbage
handful of finely chopped kale
2.5 cm (1 in) piece of cucumber, sliced
1 tbsp chopped dill
3 mint leaves, chopped
2 radishes, finely sliced
small handful of feta, crumbled
1 lemon wedge
2 tbsp Greek yoghurt
1 pita bread, cut in half
salt and freshly ground black pepper

1 Toss together the cabbage, kale, cucumber, dill, mint, radishes and feta, then place the lemon wedge on top and seal in a lunch box. Spoon the yoghurt into a small container, wrap the pita in cling film (plastic wrap) and store in the fridge until needed.

2 To serve, fill the pita with the salad mix and squeeze the lemon on top. Spoon over the Greek yogurt and season.

That time in the afternoon where the snacker in all of us comes out for a while, hunting for something to carry us through to dinner, and satisfy that sugar craving as we dip into the long afternoon. The snacks in this chapter are wholesome and contain all-natural ingredients while still hitting the spot and getting us over that 4 p.m. hump.

THE AFTERNOON SLUMP

5

CHOCOLATE, BUCKWHEAT & HAZELNUT GRANOLA

GRANOLA IS JUST TOO GOOD TO RESTRICT TO BREAKFAST TIME. THIS ONE IS MADE EVEN BETTER WITH COCOA FOR THAT AFTERNOON CHOCOLATE HIT. KEEP IN A JAR ON YOUR DESK AND YOU'LL NEVER GO HUNGRY AGAIN.

VEGETARIAN | VEGAN | GLUTEN-FREE | DAIRY-FREE | REFINED-SUGAR-FREE MAKES APPROX. 1 KG (2 LB) AND 10–15 SNACK SERVINGS

300 g (10½ oz/3 cups) gluten-free rolled oats
100 g puffed buckwheat kernels
60 g (2 oz/2 cups) puffed brown rice
100 g (3½ oz/generous 2 cups) coconut chips
200 g (7 oz/generous 1½ cups) whole hazelnuts
100 g (3½ oz/⅓ cup) pumpkin seeds
pinch of sea salt
180 g (6 oz/¾ cup) coconut oil
140 g (5 oz/½ cup) clear honey
7 tbsp coconut sugar
5 tsp cocoa powder
2 tsp vanilla extract
2 egg whites

1 Preheat the oven to 180°C (350°F/ Gas 4). Line a large baking tray with baking parchment.

2 Combine the oats, buckwheat, puffed brown rice, coconut, hazelnuts, pumpkin seeds and salt in a large bowl.

3 In a small saucepan, over a low heat, whisk together the coconut oil, honey, coconut sugar, cocoa powder and vanilla until smooth. Pour the wet mixture over the dry ingredients and thoroughly combine.

4 In a small bowl, whisk the egg whites until frothy and stir through the granola mixture. This will help to form clusters.

5 Press the mixture into the baking tray and bake for 15 minutes, or until the granola has stuck together. Roughly break up into large chunks and bake for a further 10 minutes, to crisp up the clusters.

5 Remove from the oven, and leave to cool. Store in an airtight jar or large lunch box to transport to work, and keep in a cool, dry place. Best eaten within 2 weeks.

MATCHA, ALMOND & RASPBERRY BLISS BALLS

PERFECT TO MAKE ON THE WEEKEND IN PREPARATION FOR THE WEEK AHEAD (IF THEY AREN'T ALL CONSUMED BY SUNDAY NIGHT).

VEGETARIAN| GLUTEN-FREE | DAIRY-FREE REFINED-SUGAR-FREE | MAKES 20 BALLS

120 g (4 oz/scant ½ cup) coconut oil

200 g (7 oz/generous ½ cup) clear honey

300 g (11 oz/2 cups) raw whole almonds

150 g (4½ oz/scant 1 cup) pistachios

260 g (9¼ oz/scant 3 cups) desiccated coconut

70 g (2¼ oz/generous ⅓ cup) dried dates

3 tsp matcha powder

2 tbsp almond butter

1 tsp vanilla extract

pinch of sea salt

4 tsp freeze-dried raspberries, plus 1 tbsp for decoration

1 In a small saucepan over a low heat, melt together the coconut oil and honey. Remove from the heat, and set aside.

2 In a food processor, combine the almonds, pistachios, 160 g (5¾ oz/1⅔ cups) of the desiccated coconut, dates, matcha powder, almond butter, vanilla extract and salt. Pour over the melted coconut oil and honey, and blitz on high speed until the nuts are roughly ground down, but still chunky and the mixture sticks together. Add the freeze-dried raspberries and pulse until they are dispersed throughout the mixture.

3 In a small bowl, toss together the remaining coconut and freeze-dried raspberries.

4 Line a small baking tray with baking parchment. Take heaped tablespoons of the mixture and roll into 20 equal-sized balls. Coat in the coconut and raspberry mixture and place on the lined tray.

5 Leave in the fridge for 4 hours or overnight to set. Store in a lunch box to transport to work. Lasts for up to 1 week in the fridge.

BAKED SESAME & SOY KALE CRISPS

A SALTY CHIP THAT TICKS ALL THE BOXES. CRISP AND CRUNCHY, IT'S HARD TO RESIST THESE STRAIGHT OUT OF THE OVEN, EVEN FOR A KALE SKEPTIC.

VEGETARIAN | VEGAN | GLUTEN-FREE | DAIRY-FREE | MAKES 2–3 SNACK PORTIONS

175 g (6 oz/4½ cups) kale, stems removed, leaves torn into chunks
90 ml (3 fl oz) sesame oil
3 tbsp soy sauce
2 tbsp sesame seeds

1 Preheat the oven to 200°C (400°F/ Gas 6). Line a baking tray with baking parchment.

2 Wash the kale, and dry thoroughly with a tea towel. Lay the kale out on the lined baking tray. Mix together the sesame oil and soy sauce, then pour over the kale and toss until well covered. Sprinkle over the sesame seeds. Bake for 15 minutes or until the leaves are crisp tossing halfway and taking care not to burn them.

3 Store in an airtight container. Best eaten within 2 days.

ALMOND BUTTER & CACAO NIB COOKIES

NOT YOUR CLASSIC COOKIE, BUT THE PERFECT SUBSTITUTE TO GIVE YOU THE DELICIOUS SNACK YOU'VE BEEN CRAVING ALL DAY, WITH NO HARM DONE!

VEGETARIAN | GLUTEN-FREE | DAIRY-FREE | REFINED-SUGAR-FREE | MAKES 12 COOKIES

250 g (8¾ oz/1 cup) almond butter
150 g (5¼ oz/scant ½ cup) clear honey
1 large egg
1 tsp pure vanilla extract
120 g (4 oz/scant 1¼ cups) ground almonds
1 tsp bicarbonate of soda (baking soda)
50 g (1¾ oz/scant ½ cup) cacao nibs
½ tsp sea salt

1 Preheat the oven to 180°C (350°F/ Gas 4). Line 2 baking trays with baking parchment.

2 In a medium bowl using a hand-held electric mixer, beat together the almond butter, honey, egg and vanilla extract until smooth (about 1 minute).

3 Beat in the ground almonds and bicarbonate of soda until combined. Stir in the cacao nibs.

4 Roll the dough into 12 balls, place onto the lined trays and gently press down into cookie shapes. Bake in the oven for 10 minutes or until the cookies are a light golden brown.

5 Once out of the oven, immediately sprinkle salt on top of the cookies, then leave to cool on the baking tray for 10 minutes. Transfer to a wire rack to cool completely. Store in an airtight container at room temperature. Best eaten within 5 days.

SQUASH & SMOKED PAPRIKA HUMMUS

MAKE ON THE WEEKEND FOR THE WEEK AHEAD, AS THE FLAVOURS DEVELOP OVER TIME.

VEGETARIAN | VEGAN | GLUTEN-FREE | DAIRY-FREE | MAKES 3–4 SNACK SIZED PORTIONS

500 g (1 lb 2 oz/3⅓ cups) butternut squash, peeled and cut into small pieces
2 garlic cloves
80 ml (2½ fl oz) olive oil
400 g (14 oz) can chickpeas (garbanzo beans), drained and rinsed
2 tsp smoked paprika
1 tbsp tahini
juice of 1 lemon
2 tbsp olive oil
1 tbsp pumpkin seeds, to garnish
salt and freshly ground black pepper

TO SERVE
crackers or vegetables crudités

1 Preheat the oven to 200°C (400°F/Gas 6). Line a roasting tray with baking parchment, and lay the squash and garlic cloves on it. Drizzle over 3 tablespoons of the olive oil with a generous pinch of salt and pepper, and toss both together. Roast in the oven for 20 minutes or until the squash is tender and caramelised and the garlic is soft.

2 In a food processor, combine the roasted squash and garlic cloves, chickpeas, paprika, tahini, lemon juice and remaining olive oil. Blitz until smooth (adding more oil to loosen if necessary). Season to taste.

3 Store in a container in the fridge, and serve with a garnish of pumpkin seeds and a choice of crackers or vegetable crudités.

VEGAN BERRY CRUMBLE CAKES

THESE MUFFINS ARE PACKED WITH NATURAL INGREDIENTS AND UNREFINED SWEETNESS KEEPING YOU FUELLED THROUGH YOUR AFTERNOON LOW.

VEGETARIAN | VEGAN | GLUTEN-FREE | DAIRY-FREE | REFINED-SUGAR-FREE
MAKES 12

FOR THE CRUMBLE
115 g (4 oz/scant ½ cup) coconut oil
80 ml (2½ fl oz) almond milk
200 g (7 oz/1⅔ cups) gluten-free plain (all-purpose) flour
250 g (8¾ oz/2 cups) ground almonds
150 g (5¼ oz/generous ⅔ cup) coconut sugar
½ tsp salt
140 g (5 oz/scant 1 cup) whole almonds, roughly chopped
4 tsp coconut chips

FOR THE CAKES
250 g (8¾ oz/1 cup) coconut oil
200 ml (7 fl oz) almond milk
2 tsp vanilla extract
300 g (10½ oz/generous 2½ cups) gluten-free plain (all-purpose) flour
100 g (3½ oz/1 cup) ground almonds
240 g (8½ oz/generous 1 cup) coconut sugar
1½ tsp baking powder
½ tsp salt
250 g (8¾ oz/1⅔ cup) fresh mixed berries

1 Preheat the oven to 180°C (350°F/Gas 4). Line a 12-hole muffin tin with paper cases.

2 To make the crumble, place the coconut oil and almond milk in a small saucepan over a low heat until the oil melts. In a separate bowl, stir together the remaining crumble ingredients.

3 Pour the melted coconut oil mixture on top of the dry ingredients, and stir together until it forms a crumbly texture. Set aside.

4 Make the cake base by melting together the coconut oil and almond milk, then stirring in the vanilla extract. In a separate bowl, stir together the remaining cake mixture, except for the mixed berries.

5 Pour the melted coconut oil mixture over the dry ingredients and whisk to combine. Pour the cake batter into the muffin tin, filling three-quarters of the way up. Top each cake with a small tablespoon of the berries, and spoon the crumble mixture on top.

6 Bake in the oven for 20 minutes or until golden on top and an inserted skewer comes out clean. Leave to cool in the tin, then gently remove once completely cooled. Store in an airtight container in the fridge. Best eaten within 5 days.

Packets and cans from the kitchen cupboard finally
have their time to shine. With the basic staples
at hand, you're never shy of a nourishing lunch.
The recipes are based on classic kitchen ingredients,
which are given a new lease on life.

ODDS AND ENDS

SUMAC CARROT & LENTIL SALAD

THIS RECIPE IS DEDICATED TO ALL THOSE BAGS OF BULK-BOUGHT CARROTS THAT ARE EAGERLY AWAITING THEIR USE.

VEGETARIAN | GLUTEN-FREE
MAKES 2 LUNCH PORTIONS

FOR THE SALAD

600 g (1 lb 5 oz) carrots, peeled, halved and quartered
2 red onions, cut into wedges
1 tbsp sumac
4 tbsp olive oil
250 g (8¾ oz/2½ cups) cooked puy lentils
100 g (3½ oz/2 cups) spinach
2 tbsp pomegranate seeds
2 tbsp fresh mint, roughly chopped
2 tbsp fresh parsley, roughly chopped
70 g (2½ oz/scant ½ cup) whole almonds, roughly chopped
salt and freshly ground black pepper

FOR THE DRESSING

50 g (1¾ oz/scant ¼ cup) Greek yoghurt
juice of 2 lemons
1 garlic clove, minced
2 tbsp olive oil

1 Preheat the oven to 200°C (400°F/ Gas 6). Line a baking tray with baking parchment.

2 On the tray, toss together the carrots, onions, sumac and olive oil and season generously. Roast in the oven for 20 minutes or until golden and caramelised, turning the vegetables halfway through.

3 In the lunch boxes, toss together the lentils and spinach, and arrange the roast carrots and onions on top. Sprinkle over the pomegranate, mint, parsley and almonds. Store in the fridge.

4 To make the dressing, place all the ingredients in a screw-top lidded jar, shake until well combined, and season to taste. Store in the fridge and spoon over the salad just before serving.

MOROCCAN AUBERGINE & CHICKPEA TAGINE

FOR A DISTINCT SMOKY FLAVOUR, YOU CAN FRY SOME CHORIZO AT THE BEGINNING, THEN SAUTÉ THE ONIONS IN THE CHORIZO OIL AND STIR IN LATER WITH THE AUBERGINE. THIS DISH GATHERS MORE FLAVOUR EACH DAY IT SITS, SO MAKE AHEAD FOR THE WEEK, OR EVEN FREEZE.

VEGETARIAN | MAKES 4 LUNCH PORTIONS

2 tbsp olive oil
1 red onion, diced
2 garlic cloves, minced
1½ tbsp cumin seeds
1½ tbsp smoked paprika
2 tbsp ras el hanout paste
2 large aubergines (eggplants), sliced
    into rounds,
2 red (bell) peppers, sliced lengthways
400 g (14 oz) tin chickpeas (garbanzo
    beans), drained
2 x 400 g (14 oz) tins chopped
    tomatoes
3 tomatoes, diced
55 g (2 oz/scant ⅓ cup) dried apricots,
    halved
55 g (2 oz/scant ¼ cup) dried and
    pitted dates
juice of 1 lemon
1 tsp ground cinnamon
250 ml (8½ fl oz) vegetable stock
2 tbsp roughly chopped mint
2 tbsp roughly chopped parsley

TO SERVE
couscous
Greek yoghurt
flaked almonds, toasted

1 Heat a flameproof tagine pot, or large deep frying pan (skillet) with the olive oil over a medium heat. Add the onion and cook for 2 minutes. Stir in the garlic along with all the spices, and cook for a further 2 minutes, until aromatic.

2 Add the aubergine, peppers and chickpeas to the pan and coat in the spice mix. Cook for 5 minutes.

3 Pour in the tinned and fresh tomatoes, apricots, dates, lemon juice (leaving the squeezed rind of the lemon in the sauce to infuse), cinnamon, and stock. Leave to simmer for 15–20 minutes, until thick. Stir in the mint and parsley.

4 Portion into airtight lunch boxes on top of the couscous, setting the Greek yoghurt and flaked almonds aside in separate containers ready for assembly. Alternatively, freeze, defrosting in the fridge overnight before lunch. To serve, reheat in the microwave until warmed through, and garnish with Greek yoghurt and flaked almonds.

TENDERSTEM BROCCOLI & CHILLI SPAGHETTI

THIS RECIPE CELEBRATES THE BEAUTY OF A SIMPLE PASTA DISH. NO NEED TO DROWN IT IN SAUCE, JUST LET THE FLAVOURS SPEAK FOR THEMSELVES.

VEGETARIAN
MAKES 2 LUNCH PORTIONS

200 g (7 oz) brown rice spaghetti
(or any spaghetti you have in
your cupboard)
3 tbsp olive oil, plus extra for drizzling
3 slices of day-old sourdough bread,
blitzed into breadcrumbs
1 tsp chilli flakes
30 g (1 oz/scant ½ cup) pine nuts
85 g (3 oz/generous ¾ cup) Parmesan,
grated, plus extra to serve
200 g (7 oz) tenderstem broccoli,
trimmed and halved lengthways
1 garlic clove, minced
1 long red chilli, deseeded and finely
sliced
juice of 1 lemon
salt and freshly ground black pepper
lemon wedges, to serve

1 Bring a medium saucepan of salted water to the boil. Cook the spaghetti according to the packet instructions until al dente. Drain and toss in a drizzle of olive oil to stop the spaghetti from sticking.

2 Heat 1 tablespoon of the oil in a medium frying pan (skillet), add the breadcrumbs, chilli, pine nuts and a pinch of salt to the pan, cook until the breadcrumbs are golden and crispy. Stir in the Parmesan, then tip the mixture into a small bowl and set aside. Return the pan to the heat and heat the remaining oil in the pan. Add the broccoli, garlic and chilli, and cook for 5 minutes, or until the broccoli is tender.

3 Add the cooked spaghetti to the pan, along with the breadcrumb mixture and lemon juice, and toss to combine,

4 Portion the pasta into lunch boxes and store in the fridge. Reheat in the microwave until warmed through. Serve with an extra wedge of lemon, an additional drizzle of olive oil and grated Parmesan. Lasts up to 3 days in the fridge.

KALE SALAD WITH APPLE, PECANS & EGG

A QUICK, THROW-TOGETHER SALAD, WHICH CAN EASILY BE PIMPED WITH EXTRAS ON HAND, SUCH AS A GARNISH OF HERBS, OR LEFTOVER ROAST CHICKEN.

VEGETARIAN | GLUTEN-FREE | DAIRY-FREE
MAKES 2 LUNCH PORTIONS

2 large eggs
80 g (3 oz/ 2 cups) kale, chopped
½ red apple, finely sliced
1 avocado, peeled, stoned and diced
40 g (1½ oz/scant ½ cup) pecans,
   roughly chopped

FOR THE DRESSING
½ tsp Dijon mustard
1 tbsp mayonnaise
½ lemon juice
1 garlic clove, minced
1 tbsp olive oil
salt and freshly ground black pepper

1 Place the eggs in a small saucepan and cover with cold water. Bring to the boil, then reduce to a simmer and cook for 7 minutes until hard-boiled. Immediately drain and run under cold water to stop the eggs from cooking.

2 Portion out the kale between 2 lunch boxes, arrange the apple and avocado on top, and sprinkle over the pecans. Peel and quarter the eggs, and add to each of the salads. Store in the fridge.

3 Make the dressing by stirring together the mustard, mayonnaise, lemon juice, garlic and olive oil, and season to taste. Store in an airtight jar or small container in the fridge and spoon over the salads just before serving.

SMOKY PAPRIKA BAKED BEANS ON GARLIC TOAST

ONCE YOU'VE MADE BAKED BEANS FROM SCRATCH, YOU'LL NEVER LOOK AT THE SUPERMARKET ONES IN THE SAME WAY. AS A BONUS, THIS TASTES EVEN BETTER THE NEXT DAY. YOU CAN SERVE THESE ON FRESH SLICES OF SOURDOUGH TO ADD A CRUNCH TO YOUR LUNCH.

VEGETARIAN | VEGAN | DAIRY-FREE
MAKES 4 LUNCH PORTIONS

2 tbsp olive oil, plus extra for drizzling
1 brown onion, finely diced
3 garlic cloves, finely sliced
1 tbsp smoked paprika
2 tbsp brown sugar
2 tbsp white wine vinegar
150 g (5¼ oz/1⅔ cups) button
    mushrooms, sliced
2 × 400 g (14 oz) tins chopped
    tomatoes
400 g (14 oz) tin cannellini beans
400 g (14 oz) tin haricot beans
8 sprigs of thyme, leaves only
2 tbsp parsley leaves
8 slices of sourdough bread
1 lime, cut into wedges, to serve

1 Heat the oil in a medium saucepan, add the onion and two-thirds of the garlic and sauté for 5 minutes.

2 Stir in the paprika, sugar, vinegar and mushrooms. Then add the tomatoes, beans and thyme. Simmer for 20 minutes or until the sauce has thickened. Stir in the fresh parsley.

3 The beans can be frozen at this point. Portion between containers and freeze. Defrost in the fridge overnight before serving. If not freezing, store the beans in lunch boxes in the fridge.

4 To serve, reheat the beans in the microwave until heated through. Toast the bread until crisp and firm, then rub on the remaining garlic. Drizzle over a little olive oil then spoon the beans on top. Serve with a wedge of lime.

(IMAGE ON FOLLOWING PAGES)

LIGHT & CREAMY GREEN SPELT PENNE PASTA

CRISPY BACON CAN BE ADDED FOR EXTRA FLAVOUR. ADDITIONAL GREEN VEGETABLES CAN ALSO BE TOSSED THROUGH TO MAKE YOUR MEAL EVEN MORE NOURISHING.

VEGETARIAN
MAKES 2–3 LUNCH PORTIONS

200 g (7 oz) spelt penne
1½ tbsp ricotta
1½ tbsp Greek yoghurt
1 avocado, peeled, stoned and diced
100 g (3½ oz/⅔ cup) fresh shelled peas
2 tbsp roughly chopped mint
50 g (1¾ oz/⅓ cup) pistachios, roughly chopped
50 g (1¾ oz/generous 1 cup) rocket (arugula)
salt and freshly ground black pepper

1 In a medium saucepan of salted water, bring the penne to the boil, then reduce to a simmer and cook according to the packet instructions until al dente. Drain, rinse in cold water and return to the saucepan.

2 Stir through the ricotta and yoghurt. Then toss in the avocado, peas, mint, pistachio, rocket and season.

3 Portion into lunch boxes and store in the fridge. Best enjoyed cold as a 'salad'.

A 'little of this' and a 'little bit of that' from last night's meal will become the Cinderella of lunches. Here's a chance to finally use up the back-of-the fridge ingredients, using recipes that are versatile and easily adaptable to the leftovers at hand.

LEFTOVERS MADE OVER

LEFTOVER RICE

PERSIAN SQUASH & NUT RICE SALAD

*IN THIS RECIPE, SQUASH CAN
BE REPLACED WITH ANY STARCHY
VEGETABLE AND YOU CAN USE
ANY NUTS YOU HAVE AVAILABLE.*

**VEGETARIAN | GLUTEN-FREE | DAIRY-FREE
MAKES 2 LUNCH PORTIONS**

500 g (1 lb 2 oz/3⅓ cups) butternut
   squash, peeled and cut into
   small pieces
1 red onion, cut into wedges
1 tbsp cumin seeds
3 tbsp olive oil
50 g (1¾ oz/scant ½ cup) walnuts
40 g (1½ oz/scant ⅓ cup) pistachios
30 g (1 oz/generous ¼ cup) hazelnuts
250 g (8¾ oz/1⅓ cups) cooked basmati
   or wild rice
30 g (1 oz/¼ cup) sultanas
   (golden raisins)
40 g (1½ oz/¼ cup) pomegranate seeds
40 g (1½ oz/⅓ cup) mixed seeds
2 tbsp roughly chopped coriander
   (cilantro) leaves
2 tbsp roughly chopped mint
2 tbsp roughly chopped parsley

FOR THE DRESSING
juice of ½ orange
1 tbsp clear honey
1 tsp sumac
4 tbsp olive oil
salt and freshly ground black pepper

1 Preheat the oven to 200°C (400°F/
Gas 6). Line a roasting tray with
baking parchment.

2 On the lined tray, toss together the
butternut squash, onions, cumin seeds
and olive oil. Season well. Roast in
the oven for 20 minutes (turning
halfway through) or until tender
and caramelised.

3 Roughly chop the nuts and toast in
a dry frying pan (skillet), until just
golden and fragrant. Pour into a bowl
to cool.

2 Make the dressing by stirring
together the orange juice, honey,
sumac and olive oil, season to taste,
and store in the fridge in an airtight
jar or small container.

3 To arrange the salad, toss together
the rice with the roasted vegetables,
nuts, sultanas, pomegranate, mixed
seeds and herbs, and portion into
lunch boxes. Just before serving, pour
the dressing on top, then toss to coat.

VEGETABLE & HERB PANZANELLA SALAD

FIRM AND RUSTIC BREAD WITH A CRISPY CRUST, SUCH AS SOURDOUGH, WORKS BEST IN THIS SALAD. YOU CAN CUSTOMISE THE PANZANELLA FLAVOURS TO SUIT THE HERBS YOU HAVE AT HAND. CURED MEATS ARE A NICE SMOKY ADDITION.

VEGETARIAN | DAIRY-FREE
MAKES 2–3 LUNCH PORTIONS

4 slices of stale bread, cut into rough
   cubes
80 ml (2½ fl oz) olive oil
300 g (10½ oz) mixed tomatoes, cut
   into wedges
100 g (3½ oz) roasted (bell) peppers,
   sliced
1 red onion, finely sliced
2 tbsp capers in brine
large handful of basil, roughly chopped
1 tbsp red wine vinegar
salt and freshly ground black pepper

1 Preheat the oven to 150°C (300°F/Gas 2). Line a roasting tin with baking parchment.

2 Lay the bread out on the lined tray, drizzle over 3 tablespoon of the olive oil, and salt and leave to dry out in the oven for 15 minutes. Set aside to cool.

3 In a medium bowl, toss together the cooled bread, tomatoes, peppers, onion, capers and basil. Drizzle over the vinegar and remaining olive oil, and season to taste.

4 Portion into lunch boxes, and store in the fridge. Best eaten within 2 days.

CAJUN-SPICED SWEET POTATO & QUINOA FRITTERS

ANY SMALL COOKED GRAIN AT HAND WOULD BE SUITABLE FOR THE FRITTERS AND COURGETTES CAN BE USED INSTEAD OF CARROTS.

VEGETARIAN | MAKES 8 FRITTERS

4 medium sweet potatoes, finely cubed
90 ml (3 fl oz) olive oil plus extra for
    frying
1½ tbsp cajun spice
2 garlic cloves, minced
2 carrots, grated
4 spring onions (scallions), sliced
300 g (10½ oz/1½ cups) cooked quinoa
2 tbsp roughly chopped coriander
    (cilantro) leaves, plus extra to garnish
1 tbsp snipped chives
85 g (3 oz/⅔ cup) plain (all-purpose)
    flour
1 large egg, lightly beaten
salt and freshly ground black pepper
salad leaves, to serve

FOR THE MINT YOGHURT DRESSING

65 g (2¼ oz/scant ½ cup) natural
    yoghurt
2 tbsp finely chopped mint
1 tbsp lime juice

1 Preheat the oven to 200°C (400°F/ Gas 6). Line a baking tray with baking parchment. Coat the sweet potatoes in 3 tablespoons of the olive oil and the cajun spice and season generously. Roast for 15 minutes or until tender.

2 Heat 1 tablespoon of the olive oil in a frying pan (skillet) over a medium heat. Cook the garlic for 1 minute, then add the carrots and spring onions. Cook until the carrots have softened slightly.

3 In a bowl, mash the roasted sweet potato and stir in the cooked quinoa, carrot mixture, coriander, chives, flour, egg and seasoning. Shape into 10 fritters.

4 Heat the remaining olive oil in a non-stick frying pan (skillet) over a medium-high heat. Cook the fritters in batches until they're golden and crispy, adding more oil to the pan if they start to stick. Drain the cooked fritters on kitchen paper.

5 To make the dressing, combine all the ingredients together in a bowl. Season.

6 Portion the fritters into lunch boxes, with the dressing in a separate pot. Refrigerate. Reheat them in the microwave until warmed through, Serve with the dressing and salad.

LEFTOVER POULTRY AND LEAFY GREENS

VIETNAMESE CHICKEN LEAF CUPS WITH NAM JIM SAUCE

THIS 'ASSEMBLE UPON ARRIVAL' METHOD MAKES THIS LUNCH PICNIC-FRIENDLY.

GLUTEN-FREE | DAIRY-FREE
MAKES 2 LUNCH PORTIONS

1 carrot, peeled into ribbons
15 cm (6 in) piece of cucumber, peeled into ribbons
2 tbsp rice wine vinegar
juice of ½ lime
50 g (1¾ oz/scant ½ cup) vermicelli noodles
1 baby Cos lettuce, leaves separated
250 g (8¾ oz/1½ cups) cooked chicken, shredded
50 g (1¾ oz/generous ½ cup) beansprouts
2 tbsp salted peanuts
2 tbsp chopped coriander (cilantro)

FOR THE NAM JIM SAUCE
2 tbsp soy sauce
2 tbsp groundnut (peanut) oil
½ tsp Thai fish sauce
juice of ½ lime

1 garlic clove, minced
½ long red chilli, deseeded and finely diced
1 tbsp finely chopped fresh ginger
2 spring onions (scallions), finely sliced

1 Place the carrot and cucumber in a medium bowl, pour over the vinegar and lime juice, then set aside for 10 minutes to pickle.

2 Place the vermicelli in a medium bowl, cover in boiling water, and leave for 5 minutes. Drain, rinse and set aside.

3 Make the sauce by stirring together all the ingredients.

4 To transport, pack all the elements (lettuce, vermicelli, chicken, pickled vegetables, beansprouts, peanuts, coriander and nam jim sauce) into small containers or bags, and then place in one large lunch box. Store in the fridge.

5 To serve, lay out the lettuce cups, arrange the vermicelli, chicken, pickled vegetables on top, and garnish with beansprouts, peanuts and coriander. Spoon over the nam jim sauce just before serving.

CAULIFLOWER & PARSNIP SAVOURY ALMOND CRUMBLE

*ANY LEFTOVER COOKED VEGETABLES
WILL SUIT A SAVOURY CRUMBLE
PERFECTLY. EATING IT FEELS
LIKE CRISP DAYS ALL WRAPPED
UP IN A BLANKET.*

VEGETARIAN | MAKES 2 LUNCH PORTIONS

500 g (1 lb 2 oz) roasted cauliflower
    and parsnip
55 g (2 oz/scant ½ cup) Cheddar,
    grated
2 tbsp clear honey, to taste (optional)
50 g (1¾ oz/scant ¼ cup) unsalted
    butter
100 g (3½ oz/generous ¾ cup) plain
    (all-purpose) flour
75 g (2¾ oz/¾ cup) oats
60 g (2 oz/1 cup) whole almonds,
    roughly chopped
6 sprigs of thyme, leaves only
2 tbsp olive oil
salt and freshly ground black pepper

1 Preheat the oven to 200°C (400°F/
Gas 6). In a 20 × 30 cm (8 × 12 in)
roasting tin, toss the leftover vegetables
with the Cheddar and honey, if using,
and season.

2 In a bowl, using your fingertips, rub
the butter into the flour. Gently stir in
the oats, almonds and thyme.

3 Sprinkle the crumble over the
vegetables, then drizzle the oil on top.
Bake in the oven for 20 minutes or
until golden and the vegetables are
heated through.

4 Divide the crumble between airtight
lunch boxes and store in the fridge.
To serve, reheat in the microwave until
warmed through.

LEFTOVER TOMATO SAUCE
AND VEGETABLES

FILO RATATOUILLE & RICOTTA SAMOSAS

A FRIENDLY TOMATO TWIST ON THE FAVOURITE SAMOSA. ONCE YOU'VE MASTERED THE FOLDING METHOD, YOU'LL BE MAKING THEM IN YOUR SLEEP.

VEGETARIAN | MAKES 8 SAMOSAS

150 g (5¼ oz/scant ⅔ cup) ricotta
30 g (1 oz/¾ cup) kale, chopped
pinch of ground nutmeg
85 g (3 oz) filo pastry sheets
65 g (2¼ oz/generous ¼ cup) unsalted
  butter, melted
250 g (8¾ oz/1 cup) tomato or
  vegetable sauce or ratatouille
salt and freshly ground black pepper

1 Preheat the oven to 180°C (350°F/ Gas 4). In a medium bowl, stir together the ricotta, kale, nutmeg and seasoning.

2 Cut the pastry into 8 long strips, approximately 7.5 × 46 cm (3 × 18 in). Brush the strips with the melted butter, fold in half lengthways then brush again with butter.

3 Place 1 tablespoon of the ricotta mixture and 1 tablespoon tomato or vegetable sauce at the top right hand corner of the pastry sheet, leaving a border at the top.

4 Fold the top right corner to the left edge of pastry, forming a triangle. Fold the triangle back again to the right side, then back again to the left. Butter and secure the remaining pastry seam, and place the triangle, seam side down, on a lined baking tray. Brush butter on top, and bake in the oven for 15 minutes or until golden brown.

5 Once cool, place the samosas into airtight lunch boxes and store in the fridge. To serve, reheat in the microwave until warmed through. Alternatively, package the samosas into containers and freeze. Defrost in the fridge overnight and reheat in the microwave until warmed through.

PESTO, BULGUR WHEAT & ROASTED VEGETABLE TABBOULEH

IT'S A GREAT IDEA TO HAVE ROASTED VEGETABLES IN THE FRIDGE, SO ALWAYS COOK DOUBLE. THIS RECIPE WORKS WITH ANY VEGETABLES YOU HAVE AVAILABLE.

VEGETARIAN | MAKES 2–3 LUNCH PORTIONS

100 g (3½ oz/generous ½ cup) bulgur wheat
20 g (¾ oz/scant ¼ cup) flaked almonds, toasted
2 tbsp pesto (page 49)
600 g (1 lb 2 oz) leftover roasted vegetables
2 tbsp roughly chopped parsley
1 tbsp roughly chopped basil
50 g (1¾ oz/⅓ cup) feta
juice of ½ lemon
1 tbsp olive oil
salt and freshly ground black pepper

1 In a small saucepan of salted water, bring the bulgur wheat to the boil, then reduce to a simmer for 8–10 minutes or until cooked. Drain and rinse.

2 In a small, dry frying pan (skillet), toast the almonds over a low heat until golden. Pour into a bowl to cool.

3 In a medium bowl, toss together the bulgur wheat, pesto, vegetables, parsley, basil, and feta. Drizzle over the lemon juice and olive oil and season to taste.

4 Portion into lunch boxes, and store in the fridge. Serve at room temperature with a sprinkling of the almonds.

Feasting, in essence, is all about the people you enjoy it with. A chance to reconnect, socialise and nourish ourselves in the company of co-workers and friends. This chapter has recipes for both assembling lunches straight from supermarket to desk, as well as small group efforts that will bring together a well-deserved meal. Lunch envy is no new concept; having been around since we were old enough to trade food in school to get the snacks we only dreamed our parents would give us. Now this time, with a slightly more grown-up approach, the whole concept of a 'Lunch Swap' is to broaden our taste horizons and explore different flavour combinations or finally uncover the recipe you've been fantasising about for months.
It will be just as easy as it was in school, I promise, just this time with better food.

8

COMMUNAL
FEASTS

BUY AND ASSEMBLE

BEETROOT & PUY LENTIL ZA'TAR SALAD

PRE-COOKED BEETROOTS ARE AN ABSOLUTE SAVIOUR FOR A QUICK MEAL ON THE GO, WHICH ALSO GO HAND IN HAND WITH READY-COOKED PUY LENTILS. TRY TO BUILD UP YOUR 'DESK DRAWER STAPLES' WITH MULTIPLE DRESSING INGREDIENTS TO SAVE ON REGULARLY BUYING THEM.

VEGETARIAN | GLUTEN-FREE
MAKES 4 LUNCH PORTIONS

150 g (5¼ oz/generous 3 cups) rocket
   (arugula)
200 g (7 oz/2 cups) cooked puy lentils
4 pre-cooked beetroots (beets), cut
   into wedges
65 g (2¼ oz/scant ½ cup) hazelnuts,
   roughly chopped
100 g (3½ oz/⅔ cup) goat's cheese

FOR THE DRESSING
1 tbsp tahini
1½ tbsp za'tar
½ tbsp clear honey
juice of 2 lemons
1 garlic clove, minced
4 tbsp olive oil
salt and freshly ground black pepper

1 Make the dressing by whisking together all the ingredients, and season to taste.

2 To assemble the salad, lay out the rocket leaves, top with the lentils and beetroot, sprinkle over the hazelnuts and crumble the goat's cheese on top. Finish off with a generous drizzle of the dressing.

SMOKED SALMON WITH AVOCADO & GREEN LEAF SALAD

SMOKED SALMON IS SO WIDELY AVAILABLE AT SUPERMARKETS, IT'S NO WONDER IT SNUCK ITS WAY INTO THE BOOK. FEEL FREE TO GO ALL OUT WITH THE HERBS AND ADD ANY SORT OF NUT FOR EXTRA CRUNCH.

GLUTEN-FREE | DAIRY-FREE
MAKES 4 LUNCH PORTIONS

150 g (5¼ oz/generous 3 cups)
    watercress, spinach and rocket
    (arugula) mix
150 g (5¼ oz) smoked salmon
2 avocados, peeled, stoned and diced
150 g (5¼ oz) cucumber, halved and
    finely sliced
55 g (2 oz) radishes, finely sliced
2 tbsp chopped dill
2 tbsp chopped mint leaves
2 tsp sesame seeds

FOR THE DRESSING
juice of 2 limes
4 tbsp olive oil
salt and freshly ground black pepper

1 Make the dressing by whisking together all the ingredients.

2 Arrange the salad by laying out the leafy greens and salmon, top with the avocado, cucumber, radishes and sprinkle over the dill and mint. Spoon the dressing on top and scatter over the sesame seeds.

MEDITERRANEAN ANTIPASTO SHARING BOARD

THIS PLATTER IS ALL ABOUT CELEBRATING THE APPROACHING WEEKEND IN THE COMPANY OF CO-WORKERS. THESE INGREDIENTS ARE JUST SUGGESTIONS — USE WHATEVER YOU LIKE!

MAKES 4 LUNCH PORTIONS

120 g (4¼ oz/scant 1 cup) olives

150 g (5¼ oz/2½ cups) sun-dried tomatoes in oil, drained

200 g (7 oz) roasted red (bell) peppers in oil, drained

150 g (5¼ oz/1 cup) feta

2 avocados, peeled, stoned and sliced

150 g (5¼ oz/generous ⅔ cup) pesto (page 49)

200 g (7 oz) chopped vegetables (such as carrots, (bell) peppers and celery)

400 g (14 oz/2½ cups) mixed nuts

150 g (5¼ oz) radishes

100 g (3½ oz) cured meat (such as salami and prosciutto)

1 small loaf, good-quality bread

balsamic vinegar, to drizzle

Arrange all the ingredients on a large platter or in small bowls and dig in.

128 | COMMUNAL FEASTS

SHARING THE LOAD

BARLEY, HALLOUMI & PICKLED VEGETABLE SALAD

HALLOUMI IS BOUND TO DRAW A CROWD AND COMBINED WITH PICKLED VEG AND CREAMY PEARL BARLEY, YOU MAY FIND YOURSELF SHARING WITH MORE PEOPLE THAN EXPECTED.

VEGETARIAN | MAKES 4 LUNCH PORTIONS

250 g (8¾ oz/1 cup) pearl barley
2 tbsp sunflower oil
350 g (12¼ oz/2½ cups) halloumi, sliced
4 heaped tbsp parsley leaves
4 heaped tbsp basil leaves
50 g (1¾ oz/scant ½ cup) sultanas (golden raisins)
100 g (3½ oz/1⅔ cups) sun-dried tomatoes in oil, drained
90 g (3¼ oz/generous ½ cup) whole almonds, chopped and toasted
salt and freshly ground black pepper

FOR THE PICKLED VEGETABLES

1 red onion, finely sliced
10 cm (4 in) piece of cucumber, sliced
4 carrots, peeled into ribbons
2 bay leaves
5 sprigs of thyme
100 ml (3½ fl oz) white wine vinegar
2 tbsp caster (superfine) sugar
1 tsp peppercorns

FOR THE DRESSING

juice of 2 lemons
2 tbsp olive oil
salt and freshly ground black pepepr

1 To pickle the vegetables, fill a 1 litre (34 fl oz) jar with the red onion, cucumber, carrots, bay leaves and thyme sprigs. In a bowl stir together 210 ml (7 fl oz) water with the remaining ingredients and pour over the vegetables. Screw on the lid and leave in the fridge overnight.

2 To cook the barely fill a saucepan with salted water and add the barely. Bring to the boil, then reduce to a simmer, stirring regularly, for 30–45 minutes, until the barley is soft and chewy. Drain, cool and store in a container in the fridge.

3 Heat the oil in a non-stick frying pan (skillet) over a high heat. Add the sliced halloumi and fry until golden and crispy either side. Cool and store in an airtight container in the fridge.

4 To make the dressing, combine the ingredients in a small screw-top jar and store in the fridge.

5 To serve, toss together the barley, pickled vegetables, halloumi, herbs, sultanas, sun-dried tomatoes and almonds in the dressing. Season to taste.

TAHINI, PEANUT & CABBAGE SOBA NOODLE SALAD

TO MAKE THIS GLUTEN-FREE, PURCHASE SOBA NOODLES WITHOUT ANY ADDED WHEAT FLOUR.

VEGETARIAN | GLUTEN-FREE | DAIRY-FREE
MAKES 4 LUNCH PORTIONS

160 g (5¾ oz/generous 1½ cups)
   soba noodles
1 tbsp olive oil
½ red cabbage, roughly sliced
3 spring onions (scallions), sliced
1 carrot, grated
2 avocados, peeled, stoned and diced
50 g (1¾ oz/⅓ cup) salted peanuts
small bunch of coriander (cilantro),
   roughly chopped
2 tbsp finely chopped mint leaves
½ tbsp sesame seeds
lime wedges, to serve

FOR THE DRESSING
3 tbsp tahini
1 tbsp clear honey
1 tbsp finely chopped fresh ginger
1 garlic clove, minced
juice of 2 limes
2 tbsp soy sauce
1 tsp chilli flakes
3 tbsp groundnut (peanut) oil

1 Bring a saucepan of water to the boil and cook the noodles for 5 minutes or until al dente. Drain and rinse under cold water. Toss through the olive oil to stop them sticking together. Store in a container in the fridge.

2 Prepare the remaining ingredients and store in containers in the fridge.

3 To make the dressing, whisk all the ingredients together with 2 tablespoons of water in a container and store in the fridge.

3 To serve, toss the noodles together with the cabbage, spring onions, carrot, avocado, peanuts, coriander and mint. Mix in the tahini dressing. Sprinkle over the sesame seeds and serve with the lime wedges.

CLOCKWISE FROM THE TOP:
TAHINI, PEANUT & CABBAGE SOBA
NOODLE SALAD; BARLEY, HALLOUMI
& PICKLED VEGETABLE SALAD;
SUN-DRIED TOMATO & ASPARAGUS
PUFF PASTRY TART

SUN-DRIED TOMATO & ASPARAGUS PUFF PASTRY TART

POSSIBLY THE LEAST EFFORT TO PUT TOGETHER, WITH THE MOST REWARDING RESULTS. THE MASCARPONE CAN BE SUBSTITUTED FOR ANY SOFT CHEESE AVAILABLE SUCH AS RICOTTA OR CREAM CHEESE.

VEGETARIAN
MAKES 4 LUNCH PORTIONS

375 g (13¼ oz) ready rolled puff pastry
1 large egg, beaten
100 g (3½ oz) asparagus
1 tbsp olive oil
zest of 1 lemon
200 g (7 oz/scant 1 cup) mascarpone
   cheese
200 g (7 oz/1⅓ cups) feta
100 g (3½ oz/1⅔ cups) sun-dried
   tomatoes in oil, drained
2 tbsp pesto (page 49)
4 tsp pine nuts, toasted
salt and freshly ground black pepper

1 Preheat the oven to 200°C (400°F/ Gas 6). Line a baking tray with baking parchment. Place the pastry onto the tray and score a 2 cm (¾ in) border around the edge. Brush over the beaten egg, then make fork indents all over the inside of the border. Bake for 10 minutes, until golden and puffed. Store in an airtight container, in a cool, dark, dry place.

2 Line another baking tray with baking parchment. Place the asparagus onto the tray, drizzle over the olive oil and lemon zest and season. Roast for 10 minutes, until tender. Allow to cool then store in an airtight container in the fridge.

3 Portion out the cheeses into containers and store in the fridge until ready to use.

4 To assemble, spread the mascarpone over the pastry, and sprinkle over the feta. Arrange the sun-dried tomatoes and asparagus on top, dollop on the pesto, then sprinkle over the pine nuts. Season and cut into slices to serve.

INDEX

THANK YOU

First of all, the biggest of all thank you to Kajal Mistry and Kate Pollard for having a vision and trusting me with it. It was such an honour and a truly surreal couple of months putting the book together – its been the biggest blast! Another massive thank you to Fred for her beautiful design and the Hardie Grant team for all their hard work bringing the book together.

Rosa for all her amazing hard work and laughs over the shoot days, and India for also being the most incredible help.

Mum, Dad, and Katrina all the way back home in Australia, for wholeheartedly supporting me from afar over many Skype calls discussing the complexities of dhal, the pure beauty of couscous, and reading first drafts. Your encouragement and excitement continued to spur me on with so much enthusiasm.

My adopted family at Franze and Evans, London; Teresa, Emma, Connie, Nico and all the other hilarious guys and gals on the team for sharing a common love for lunch.

Everyone else I met in London, who shared such a love for the good things in life (aka food) I'm so lucky to have your support. Tons of hugs and thank yous to Milli, Sanchia, and Kaiva.

ABOUT THE AUTHOR

Bec Dickinson is a cake baker, food stylist, photographer and blogger currently based in Melbourne. The 21-year-old has made a love for good food into a living, working for caterers, cafes and also alongside photographers. Bec documents her labours of love on her food blog *Daisy and the Fox* through the eyes of her trusty Canon camera.

LOVE YOUR LUNCHES by Bec Dickinson

First published in 2017 by Hardie Grant Books

Hardie Grant Books (UK)
52–54 Southwark Street
London SE1 1UN
hardiegrant.co.uk

Hardie Grant Books (Australia)
Ground Floor, Building 1
658 Church Street
Melbourne, VIC 3121
hardiegrant.com.au

British Library Cataloguing-in-Publication Data.
A catalogue record for this book is available from
the British Library.

ISBN: 978-1-78488-095-8

Publisher: Kate Pollard
Senior Editor: Kajal Mistry
Editorial Assistant: Hannah Roberts
Photographer: Bec Dickinson
Art Direction: Friederike Huber
Illustrations: Esme Lonsdale
Copy editor: Jane Bamforth
Indexer: Cathy Heath
Production: Stephen Lang and Vincent Smith
Colour Reproduction by p2d

Printed and bound in China by 1010

10 9 8 7 6 5 4 3 2 1